Heartfelt Praise for
The Realness of a Woman

"This book is an excellent source of divine wisdom that will assist all who study and read its content. It's a reminder that when we are open to the divine flow of Life's healing, loving energy, we receive it and then give it back to others in the form of light."
—Dr. Mitch Ergas, D.C.
Author of *The Magic of Modern Day Miracles, All Women are Special,* President & Co-founder of Life Wellness & Chiropractic, PC, Smyrna, GA

"As a creative being, my hope is to raise the level of love within each individual I encounter so that they can be a living gift to themselves and others. Discovering *The Realness of a Woman* was a gift to myself that was a spiritual book-end to 'The Cinderella Complex.' A warm, embracing read for every woman 15 - 99."
—Sara Hickman
Producer, Songwriter, Singer, Creator of musical audios that include: *Newborn, Toddler and Big Kid,* Austin, TX

"Writing from a place of deep insight and solid experience, Dr. Porter has provided here a groundbreaking, practical book for women who want to discover, reclaim and empower the divine feminine within themselves. A must read for every modern woman."
—Colin C. Tipping
Award winning author of *Radical Forgiveness, Making Room for the Miracle,* Marietta, GA

"*The Realness of a Woman* is a concise and practical "magical mystery tour" of the secrets for having what we want while loving just being ourselves. Her honest, down-to-earth sharing is one of Carolyn's trademarks. She speaks with authority about living our Divine Essence. The instructions she gives for attracting love, in general, and for finding your best mate are sure-fire. If you want to live your life as a joyous creator, read this book!"
—Marcia Davis, M.S.W., L.C.S.W.
Psychotherapist, Personal growth consultant, Speaker, Asheville, NC

"In *The Realness of a Woman*, Carolyn awakens us to our own magnificence. Her book helps us to embrace how powerful and worthy we truly are. She shows us that the love we want in our life must start with self-love then overflow and be shared from that feeling that resides in ones own heart. This book is a true gift of love."
—**Dr. Jill Kahn**
Author of *The Gift of Taking*, Roswell, GA

"In her book *The Realness of a Woman*, Dr. Carolyn Porter has her hand on the pulse of addressing and resolving women's issues. This book has the tools for living in the now, moving forward, and growing in the One Truth. 'Where energy goes power flows.' Choose to create your power. Great job!!!"
—**Rev. Dr. Reginald Worrell, Jr.**
Author of *The Chosen People are the Ones Who Choose*, President of Universal Brotherhood University, Stone Mountain, GA

"Like a seasoned sherpa, Carolyn Porter's book leads the reader across the difficult terrain of life and relationships on a path anyone can easily follow. She covers chakras, for example, in the most concise way imaginable leaving their power exposed for easy integration into a greater understanding of our potential as humans. She sees us reaching for love, which is our natural state, and finding it on the other side of barriers we've accumulated since childhood. An excellent work offering guidance for men as well as the women for whom it is written."
—**Bob Keeton**
Living Successfully Radio Host, Richmond, VA

"*The Realness of a Woman* is a powerful, inspiring and practical book. It's a treasure of principles, spiritual tools, practical techniques, and empowerment activities that can change your life. A tremendous self-help book packed with ideas that will show you how to choose nothing but the best."
—**Helene Hamilton**
Principal and Founder of New Vistas Academy-College Preparatory, Brooklyn, NY

"Refreshing, witty and wise. Full of genuine and useful insights for achieving what you want. In this extraordinary book each chapter reveals gems of understanding that nourish your soul and being. What is it that makes this book really powerful? Each chapter ends with a summary of the major points, followed by a simple exercise for a personal application to your own life and then an affirmation to sustain the learning. Dramatic changes start happening at an amazing pace."

—Ruth Zanes
Author of *Mini Motivators,* Success Coach, Speaker, Owner of Unlimited Resources, Inc., Alpharetta, GA

"This masterpiece of practical and spiritual wisdom is the perfect companion for women at all levels of consciousness - from those just awakening to their "realness," to those who are seeking to put wings to their wholeness. As a spiritual mentor and group facilitator, I consider this book to be an invaluable guide and companion for journeys into oneself on the deepest levels, and for the empowerment that comes with such knowledge."

—Reverend Deborah Smith, M.A., C.Ht.
Founder and Spiritual leader of Unity Spirit - a center for spiritual growth and pastoral care, Richmond, VA

"From beginning to end this book is a wonderful playground of ideas and inspirations for anyone who truly desires more joy in living!"

—Matt ParClair, Ph.D.
Associate Minister of Unity North Atlanta Church, Marietta, GA

Published by Empower Productions
205 Ridgepoint Court
Woodstock, Georgia 30188

First printing November 2003

Library of Congress: 2003097205

ISBN: 0-9711150-2-8

Printed by Worzalla
3535 Jefferson Street
Stevens Point, WI 54481
www.worzalla.com

Cover art and photograph by Mande Porter
Illustrations by Mande Porter and Deborah Porter
Book design by Jill Balkus
Edited by Kevin Bradley

To women who are seeking their true love . . .

With Appreciation

I am grateful beyond words for *Hope,* my beautiful guardian angel, and the host of *other angels* whose inspiration guided me with this writing, for without them there would be no words.

✐

I have deep appreciation for the many *"teachers"* who showed up in my life when the time was right.

✐

I express gratitude for my beautiful daughter *Mande Cherie,* who used her artistic genius and created my cover art.

✐

It is with amazement I acknowledge the gift of two of my talented daughters, *Mande Cherie* and *Deborah Lynn,* who without any training have created all the wonderful sketches for this book.

✐

To my five children, each with their own wonderful gifts, *Stephen, Deborah, Scott, Melinda,* and *Mande,* my daughter-in-law *April,* and my grandchildren *Casey, Cory, Chandler* and *Connor,* who have blessed my life in magnanimous ways through the never-ending circle of love.

✐

With a thankful heart I acknowledge my editor, *Kevin Bradley,* who worked quickly, proficiently, and patiently with me in making these words flow with readable ease. An incredible feat!

✐

I acknowledge the friendship I share with many who with enthusiasm have been there for me as this book came to be, and for these who gave so much support: *Teri, Beverly, Maggie,* and *Ruth.*

Table of Contents

Celebration for Deanna, a Woman of Worth x
Preface xiii
Introduction xv
To the Men Who Dream for a Woman of Realness xvii

PART I: *Seeking*

Programmed Roots 1
Operational Base 11
An Illusion 27
Resistance 51
Attachment 69
Why - Because 85
Just Be 97

PART II: *Remembering*

I'm Okay 111
The Void 127
Stepping Into Your Passion 137
The Daffodil Principle 153
Remembering Your Power 163
Coincidence or Miracle? 197
Knowing Your Truth 209

PART III: *Being*

Choices 223
Life Extraordinaire 235
Playtime 247
See the Horizon 257
Your Divine Essence 269
Attracting Love 283
Reflection 304

APPENDIX

Special Invitation 309
Bibliography 310
About the Author 312
More from Carolyn Porter 313

Celebration for Deanna - A Woman of Worth

On July 13, 2003, just days after the completion of this book, Deanna, my dearest friend, transitioned from this life to the other side. Her pain is gone and she is happy as she now lives in the Light. We who are left behind feel the emptiness without her presence, but celebrate her new life of freedom from her arthritis pain. Now she can fly!

Deanna was an earth angel whose loving heart reached out to touch the souls of those who crossed her path. Words that come to mind when I think of her are: loving, giving, compassionate, supportive, understanding, honest, loyal, trusting, generous, courageous and real. When we met there was an instantaneous bond of friendship and we knew we had traveled a path together before. She's the kind of friend everyone dreams of having in a lifetime.

She held the light for me when I traveled through a dark tunnel. When it was time for her to experience a dark tunnel, I was there with a light. How many times I sat by her bed I cannot count, making her laugh or rubbing her back, and she was there holding my hand as I cried until there were no more tears, when my heart felt as if it would break. Long walks and talks as we bared our souls and shared our dreams. I'd bring her lunch or "chauffeur" her home from the hospital. The next thing you'd know a beautiful card that touched my heart would appear or there she'd be, at my door, bearing a basket of gifts she'd created with love, always with a smile.

She was my support and encourager when things felt rocky. Sometimes she'd need to talk and we might do just that 'til 2:00 am! We might connect daily or let weeks go by, but we always knew we were there for each other at any given moment, whether in laughter as silly little girls, through the sometime tears, or all that goes between. In the early days of my seminars, she and I traveled to another state so I could present a seminar. Two of my daughters and two of their friends were there to help. *No one showed up.* I was dismayed for just a moment until she quietly said, "You came here to give a seminar, so do it." So I did, for my two daughters, their two friends, and Deanna. It was a wonderful experience.

She would have been proud of this book. She often read what I wrote - my "critic." God's timing is always perfect and what better time to release this book than when she chose to go to the other side; I can share the realness of love through our friendship even though she has moved past physical form. She left a week before her fifty-first birthday, and although she never saw my gift that had been made for her, she knows. The words inscribed on the gift say it all:

> *Once in a while a friend is found*
> *Who's a friend right from the start*
> *Once in a while a friendship is made*
> *That really warms the heart*
> *Once in while a friendship is found*
> *To have a lifetime through*
> *It really does happen just once in a while...*
> *It happened to Me and You!*

We never know what the next day may bring; we only have today. It is a gift as are the friends who walk the path with you. Remember to tell them of the joy they bring into your life, for tomorrow may never come.

Deanna's physical restrictions never held her back from living life. She gave and gave from the depths of her heart to everyone; she was real, a special soul of God's design. For several years she and I provided entertainment for assisted living homes, she with her beautiful voice and me at the piano. Her new residence: Heaven - singing with the angels!

Until we meet again Deanna, know that you have brought immeasurable joy into my life. You are a Woman of Worth!

To Erica, her beloved daughter -

Your mother saw your greatness as she poured her love into you. You have been given a marvelous gift, that of being able to carry her light to the world through you. So let your light shine all over this world, and she too will shine. She is always with you, forever. You too are a Woman of Worth!

A Woman of Worth

A woman of worth, her riches beyond earthly treasure,
a heart spun with gold, reaches in touching your soul;
a flower so rare, her beauty unfolds over time.
Adorned with truth and honor,
undaunted by the wiles of worldly men,
she builds on today, fully present in the now
for futures can change in a moment.
She makes her own rules
not bound to limits placed by others;
she sees the rainbow through the storm,
standing in her own light,
needing no one to brighten the path,
she does not betray herself for anyone.

A woman of worth, embraces life's passion,
speaks gently from divine wisdom,
giving credence to the power within.
Though she may stumble,
quickly she rises with the grace of nobility.
Her heartspace open, loving and compassionate
she feeds her own soul,
not needing a boost from anyone else,
but accepting it when it is given.
Joy rises in her as her spirit soars
to enlightened spheres beyond,
she touches your heart, reaches into your soul
this woman is a gift to the world.

A woman of worth, loving herself,
shares love with those who cross her path,
for a moment, a passing space, or a lifetime.
She is priceless!

- Carolyn Porter

Preface

All of my life I sought to experience and know real love. I thought I had found it several times, even with my former husband with whom I remained for 32 years. But early in the marriage I realized I had not found true love as I thought. So I searched for answers for many years until recently when, through various happenstances, I finally came to understand the reality of real love, love without judgment and restrictions, love that forgives and surpasses human comprehension.

Finding love is the innate desire of all human beings. It is undoubtedly one of the strongest desires of every individual on this planet. Yet so few people ever experience such love. Why does it elude the vast majority of human beings? Because they do not understand the essence of real love.

More than likely you are right now thinking of romantic love between two partners, but there is so much more to love than that. Love is love between any two individuals. The response will be different with different individuals as in parent/child, friend/friend, husband/wife, but it's all love, because love is all there is.

My beliefs, and I honor yours if they are different, tell me that God created me and everyone else in this universe. This means that all of us are connected with each other and are all part of God. God is love which means each of us began as love and are love. It also means we are all intertwined in love as part of God and each other, so why do we not understand love?

We live in this world, a world of fear with negative patterns and programming, and forget from where we came. In so doing we erase our understanding of love as we once knew and try out the world's interpretation of love. In this process we find ourselves in difficult, non-nurturing and painful relationships that keep us from knowing who we really are because we are listening to earthly repetitions of love. We get lost in the quagmire of limited beliefs, losing ourselves in the thoughts of others. And we don't love ourselves which means there is no love for us to share with the people in our life. Everything in our life begins within us.

In this book I will share with you an understanding of the love we all seek as I have experienced it through earthly eyes and then eyes of the Light. Real love doesn't need to be achieved, it simply is. Once you have obtained the knowingness of love as the Universe intended us to feel, nothing in your life will ever be the same again, and you will see that the love of the world is not really love, it is *need*. This awareness can transform your life and create a passion that grows and grows, a passion for life itself as you realize the greatness within your own being. It is recognizing this greatness that already lies within you that gives you *realness* in being the wonderful woman you really are, one who is genuinely in love with herself!

Introduction

The reason for our existence in this lifetime is to allow our soul to rise to a higher vibrational level from where it is. We accomplish this through lessons and experiences that give growth into the expansive territory of the unknown. Raising our vibrational level brings us closer to the Divine Oneness we are seeking. Divine Oneness is love, for love is the essence of our natural beingness. Everything in the realm of the physical world is an illusion of the essence of love.

Our journey is for our spiritual awakening to the glorious awareness of a life of love. The more of love we become, the more intolerant we are of the ways of worldly thought. The more intolerant of worldly delusions we become, the more we realize our own greatness that is intertwined in the transformation of this planet.

In this book you will travel beyond the realm of the mind into the knowingness of your spirit. If your consciousness cannot grasp the depth of realization, that's okay. Through surrender and allowing your spirit to hold your hand and open your heart, your journey will transform you into perfect mindfulness.

This book is written for those women who seek more from life, who know they are more and are searching to be revealed. Your journey through these pages is solely to substantiate enlightenment of your soul, the place where you are real. As you read this book, yearn to understand the relevance of knowing the depth and breath of divine love, for the love you are knowing is you. Love is all there is.

The empowerment activity at the end of each chapter is simply a tool to help you on your journey. Utilizing the affirmations may assist your mind with the changes you wish to create. Everything is designed to encourage your empowerment.

For the Men Who Dream of Finding a Woman of Realness

A woman of realness is a powerful woman, who knows who she is and what she is here to do. Her main focus is love and sharing it with the world. To many men this woman is feared, for men have been programmed that they must be the power through control.

Dear men, there can be no fear. This woman will love you more deeply than any other as she helps you in your own healing. She will encourage you, support you, entice you and praise you for your own worthiness, but all the while she will not bow to you as a servant might do, for she is her own master.

This woman of realness will not possess you, binding you to expectations that could reduce you to smallness. She is complete as she is. She is on her own path as you are on yours, but together you can hold each other's hand.

A woman of realness desires a man who is willing to expand his possibilities as he supports her in her growth. There is no neediness so there is freedom from attachments. She desires that you follow your dreams no matter what they look like, so you can be complete as you are. She does not fear your growth, but welcomes it.

So men, cast away your fears and doubts for a woman of realness, for she is a great gift. She is a jewel that will sparkle more brightly over time, glowing in her own love as it reflects through you. She is a woman you can cherish. She can't let you down because you won't have expectations of her. She can't disapprove of you because you do not need her approval; you already know who you are. Neither does she need your approval for she knows her own worthiness.

Together, with two individuals who are complete alone, the joining will exemplify the power of God. The universal force shining through this connection will multiply manyfold the power of two alone. It is born of realness. It is a relationship created in heaven. It is a relationship formed of divine love that will shine its power throughout the world so that the world knows real love. Enjoy!

Seeking

PART I

Deeply etched, tightly we hold
to beliefs we've truly outgrown.
Stretch your gaze, see possibilities
that exceed the imagination.

- Carolyn Porter

1

Programmed Roots

As little girls we were usually taught that life for us should include falling in love with the "right" guy, getting married, having children, and taking care of the household duties which included being the chauffeur, cook, maid, nurse, accountant, shopping expert, time juggler, organizer, romantic partner, movie star, counselor, negotiator, gardener, all because of love. And to top it off we would do all of this within the 24 hours of each day! And in spite of the fact that we were expected to run the household our husband's were given the title of "head of the house!" You were probably taught to hold your tongue and to be respectful, pleasant, loving at all times, submissive, accepting, and always on call for whatever. We became *caretakers*! This was to be the life of Cinderella who found Prince Charming, right?

Maybe you were not part of that belief system, but most females grew up with that old thinking pattern. It came from many generations of our ancestors who only knew what they had been taught, so they simply taught what they knew. Most of us followed what we were taught and bought right into the system of patriarchal philosophy - husband, then wife, then children. Notice the wife, in the middle, wedged between the husband and children. And that's where we often stayed - wedged between needy people, trying hard to fulfill their needs. We sold our soul for love. What happened to us? At least we no longer had to walk behind our husbands as had been past custom; we had come a long way baby!

Before we proceed let me share how much I loved being a homemaker. I wanted every one of my children and was blessed to give birth to five living children with two more in heaven. They became my life, which I'm sure many of you understand, and I loved every minute of being a mom. Being a wife was enjoyable part of the time, but I found it didn't fill my needs as my perception was. In fact, my marriage was quite difficult but I bought into the belief that once married, always married, so I made the best of it that I could. I followed my duties and was respectful, pleasant and submissive as much as I could be. I am not saying that choosing this life was not good. There were so many wonderful experiences as I raised my children, and the rewards were endless. In hindsight, the valuable lessons I learned were what brought me to where I am today, and they made it possible for me to help myself and others with similar experiences.

My children were and are some of my greatest gifts in this lifetime. The problem was that as the years went by I found little true happiness, and life seemed like such an effort at times. I was restless and often miserable, which made me feel guilty because I was taught that my life would be happy if I did what was "right." Of course where there's guilt there is the fear of punishment, so I lived with that noose always hanging around my neck. What was missing was who I was. I based my identity with others.

We all had different scenarios. Perhaps your beliefs were clouded with abuse or indifference, or maybe your parents didn't want you in the first place. Maybe you were an orphan sent to live in foster homes, never feeling wanted or loved by the mother who birthed you. Perhaps the message that came through to you was that you created a problem by being born, that you were not worth much and were dispensable, and so you carried that thought with you into adulthood. Or maybe your "family" was totally dysfunctional, giving you little guidance about the values of life, all wrapped up in their own selfish needs, all striving for the attention that needy people must have to survive. Maybe you were in a family that produced so many children that you got lost in the crowd, or felt like you did.

Whatever our stories we have old beliefs that were so deeply ingrained into our minds that the programming still has its effects in our lives today. This is evident through the View Master in which we see the relationships we attract into our lives, relationships that do not help us heal and grow, but rather keep us in lack consciousness and powerless, making us feel unable to escape the self-imposed bondage of these relationships. We might ask ourselves if any relationship isn't better than none. For many women, particularly as their children are grown and moving out on their own, life becomes rather dreary as they look forward to what? Now they get to take care of a husband, or if alone try to find someone else who is a good companion, become a grandmother and fill that role, and to continue the cycle of caretaker and being needed because that's all they know.

Now let's flip the coin to the other side and notice that sometimes a more complete woman attracts to her a wonderful partner who cherishes and appreciates her and actually encourages her to be herself. But even in this kind of nurturing relationship, there can still be the tendency of one partner to dominate the other, still creating a sense of powerlessness at times. The fear of more power in one partner can underlie issues in the relationship and may sneak in through the back door unnoticed, at least initially. As we go through the information in this book, be mindful of how easy it is to get caught up in negative aspects of someone else's thought process even if you are appreciated and cherished by them.

As we continue, please understand that these thoughts are merely making you aware of unconscious patterns that invade your everyday thinking process and keep you from moving forward on your own path. This is not about bashing men, for I truly love men and cherish my relationship with each of the men in my life. Neither are these thoughts about making men feel guilty or inferior and us superior in any way. These thoughts were brought through me simply to share the fact that we lose ourselves in the process of life, the process of being mothers, wives, partners, caretakers, guardians, friends, family members and employees. We lose who we are and what our purpose on this planet is. We lose our power by allowing everyone else to control our lives and in so doing we feel safe and protected and loved. This is not love. This is simply *need*, and it has become the basis of what we humans call love. It is nothing less than bondage.

"Be a first-rate vision of yourself, not a second-rate vision of somebody else."

- Judy Garland

Review

1. Women were primarily taught to be caretakers.
*We were taught that good little girls find their Prince Charming
and live happily ever after, by taking care of him.*

2. Old programming still shows its affects in our lives today.
*We remain in relationships that are not working
because of old beliefs that we accept as truth.*

3. We have allowed everyone else to control our lives.
*We have lost our souls to the bondage of the world's
interpretation of love, which is actually need.*

Empowerment Activity

Make a list of things that would make you feel good.
Check any of the suggestions you agree with
then add additional pleasures.

___ a massage	___ a romantic night out
___ a luxurious bath	___ flowers
___ shopping	___ start a business
___ alone time	___ a facial
___ a housekeeper	___ walk in the park
___ spend time with a friend	___ a new outfit
___ a vacation	___ walk on the beach
___ dance	___ do something daring
___ go to a spa	___ a new hairdo
_____	_____
_____	_____
_____	_____

So enjoy yourself for you are worth it!

Affirmation

*I choose to let go of old limiting beliefs and
replace them with unlimited possibilities.*

Generations past said the earth was flat,
others believed women had no rights.
Don't allow your limiting beliefs
to become your truth.

                                        - Carolyn Porter

2

Operational Base

We've been discussing the role of a woman in today's society, particularly the role of a woman who is restless and seeking. Granted, some of you may not fit the scenario of wife, mother, or caretaker in the same sense, but you are undoubtedly part of the patriarchal consciousness that ruled the time surrounding our birth - the male is in charge. Even if you never married or became a mother, parts of your life reflect old programming that don't serve you anymore.

For the most part we've been operating with a base of lack and low self-worth all of our lives. We were taught our role was to be submissive to the male, and our society has propigated that consciousness for decades. Any woman in the business world knows of situations, or even has personal experiences with a situation, in which a male received more income for the same job description just because he was a male, or perhaps received a higher position for the same reason. We're all aware of stories of women who were advised to "sell" their bodies to a man in order to receive a job, promotion, more income or other "favors." We know of so many women who opt to remain in unhealthy relationships because they feel incapable of taking care of themselves, are afraid to leave, don't want to be alone, or feel trapped for one reason or another.

Why do women feel this way? Why do so many women stay in unhealthy relationships when they know deep inside that it isn't good for them to stay? Why do so many women feel inadequate or incomplete without a man in their life? Why are many women living a life that's scripted for them without thinking about what they might like their life to be? And even if you're a woman who knows you want more, why are you not out there getting it?

As I reflected on my own life and observed the patterns of many women's lives, I realized that the core issue for most women is low self-esteem. Actually, low self-esteem according to psychologists all across our country, is the number one problem in our society today. So it doesn't just affect women, but many men as well. Think about this for a moment. Low self-esteem man meets low self-esteem woman. They feel this powerful chemistry which they call love. They can't imagine ever being without each other again, so they decide to become partners, for life they say. All is well for a while. Then low self-esteem woman needs constant reminders of how much she is loved and wants her partner always with her and not out with his friends without her, in order to feel most important. After all, they couldn't stand being apart before. Low self-esteem man needs "mothering" and being taken care of while his desires are being met, that he is her protector and "idolized" by her to boost his image and therefore his self-worth. Demands from each partner begin to surface and fears of all kinds emerge. Each partner is looking for the other person to fill his/her needs and supply the lack that is within themselves. Each partner is trying to control and manipulate the other into what they need. They don't realize this of course, they just do it. It's a programmed pattern.

These patterns and beliefs were passed down to us by our parents and the generations before them. In addition, we have the beliefs of structured religion that feed the old system of a patriarchal lifestyle. Even if we do not follow that system in our daily practice, we still have those ingrained patterns in the memory of our subconscious. We must learn to recognize these patterns and through that awareness allow the release of everything that no longer serves us for our highest good. It's not an easy process and it forces us to confront things in our lives that act as barriers because we are fearful, especially when we are hiding these fears. That's why we remain where we are, because of fear, something that isn't even real but affects our *real lives*. More on this subject in the next chapter.

Our operating base has two basic parts - the desire for love and the need to survive. We've already discussed that all living creatures on this planet want love, but we've also mentioned that they are seeking love from a source that cannot supply it. Along with the desire for real love is the requirement for survival. What good would love be without survival. Since the majority of people operate their entire life from these two bases, I feel the necessity to explain how the seven chakras work and what they mean. These chakras are focused energy locations within the vortex of our bodies. They act as doorways of conscious understanding. Knowing the body's seven major energy centers will help you realize why love is so often misrepresented on this earth and why so many people never experience the one thing they seek all their life - real love.

Energy

First of all, before we can discuss the chakras and their purpose in understanding our beingness, we must realize that you and everything else in our universe is composed of energy. Energy runs through us, around us, out from us, and is continually transmitting this life force. Energy makes things happen. Once energy is created it can never be destroyed; it can change form, but can never die. Energy doesn't recognize whether something is negative or positive, it just moves and spins out whatever vibration is there. This means that if we allow negative thoughts and beliefs to enter our mind, those negative thoughts will project outward into the energy flow and create more of the same. Knowing the Law of the Universe - that what we send out is mirrored right back to us - we must be careful what we think and do. The old beliefs that are ingrained into our cells' memory are continually repeating in our thoughts enabling us to create the same pattern - positive or negative - over and over in our lives.

Since energy is so powerful and creates our life, you can see why knowing how we operate from our base makes such a big difference in what our life looks like. We must shift the energy flow from our negative programmed patterns in order to make our life what we really want, including the love we want to experience. The energy is often blocked by these outdated beliefs that keeps the individual from stepping into the possibilities their life holds for them.

Your personal energy field extends outward from your physical body. It could be as broad as your outstretched arms, but usually extends about six inches. We call this energy field the aura. The aura can be seen by some people, and even photographed when using the right camera. Auras can be white or in colors. The color or colors around you depict what is going on in your energy fields at that time and can help you understand where changes must happen to improve your life by allowing the flow of energy. Realize that this energy field around us, or aura, is projecting outward continuously what we feel and think on the inside. It's quite fascinating and if you have never experienced an aura photograph and reading, it might be fun for you as an insightful adjunct in understanding who you are.

The Seven Chakras

The main reason it is important to understand the chakras is in creating wholeness within ourselves. All aspects of ourselves - physical, mental, emotional, spiritual - must work together for each is as much a part as the other. All the energy created from our beliefs and attitudes express in a physical way. The emotional, mental and spiritual forces flow into physical expression as well, for the energy created from them runs through the chakras and is distributed to our cells, organs and tissues. This knowingness gives appreciative insight into how we create our own circumstances, whether positive or negative.

The word chakra means "wheel" which describes the chakras as spinning out energy from the corresponding area of the body. The chakras are moving, vibrating, pulsating wheels of light. The chakras are the network in which body, mind and spirit interact in our entire system. Although we contain hundreds of focused energy locations throughout our body, these are the seven major energy centers.

Each chakra center has its own characteristics and functions and corresponds to certain aspects of our mindfulness, representing a specific color. Understanding the relationship between the chakras and this mindfulness helps us to better realize ourselves.

Since our entire body/mind system connects to all universal consciousness, as one person becomes whole then on a collective level the world is closer to wholeness.

The seven major chakras are as follows, beginning from the top of our head: Crown Chakra, Third Eye, Throat, Heart, Solar Plexus, Sacral Plexus and Root Chakra. The chakras are descriptive of their relationship as the physical body is upright. Blockages in the chakras can lead to either *over* or *under* reactions in the physical realm. Let's look at each one individually so that we understand their functions and relationship to our wholeness.

Crown Chakra
Violet - has the highest vibrational rate

This chakra is the unification of the higher self with the human personality. It is Oneness with our Creator and the place from which we receive divine wisdom and understanding. Here is inspiration, selfless service and where we can perceive beyond the physical realm. Whenever we pull to us divine light or inspiration it comes through our crown chakra.

Glandular Connection: The crown chakra regulates the endocrine system due to the relationship with the pituitary gland.

Blockages: When there are blocks in the crown chakra we might find ourselves confused, depressed, lacking inspiration, feeling alienated from others or even senile.

Third Eye
Dark Blue - indigo

The third eye is where we find intuition, insightfulness, clairvoyance, peace of mind, spiritual perception, devotion and concentration. We say that when the third eye is fully open we can receive great insights into the spirit realm, that we're really connected and understand our soul's purpose. It's function relates to vision.

Glandular Connection: The third eye connection is with the pineal gland, which secretes melatonin and assists the crown chakra with hormone balance.

Blockages: Blockages in our third eye connection creates fear in our lives, tension, anxiety, headaches, lack of concentration, and bad dreams.

Throat Chakra
Blues - whole range of blues

Herein lies the power of the spoken word. This chakra gives communication with creative expression in speech, writing and all forms of the arts. We are able to integrate peace, knowledge, wisdom, honesty, truth, kindness and genuineness from this chakra. This chakra's function relates to communication and speech - sound vibrations.

Glandular Connection: The throat chakra relates to the thyroid and parathyroid glands which affect metabolism, body heat and growth.

Blockages: If there are blocks in this chakra there is lack of discernment, ignorance, depression, communication problems or knowledge used unwisely that is not for the highest good of all.

Heart Chakra
Green, also pink/rose

This is the anchor of the life-force from the Higher Self. This is our love center, pouring out unconditional love, forgiveness, compassion, understanding, acceptance, peace, openness,

contentment and a oneness with life. This is where real love emanates. From this chakra up we find love, divine oneness, and spiritual inspiration.

Glandular Connection: It is related to the thymus gland.

Blockages: When this chakra is blocked there is lack of love or love that is suppressed within the being. There will be emotional instability, heart problems and low self-worth.

Solar Plexus Chakra
Yellow and gold

The function of this chakra is to vitalize the nervous system and emotions. Here is our energy, self-control, warmth, transformation, laughter, personal power, mastery of desire, will and where we awaken to possibilities. This chakra is the ego center.

Glandular Connection: It works with the adrenal glands, working with cortisol levels and stress.

Blockages: Blockages in this chakra result in digestive problems, anger, fear, hate, and too much emphasis on power and recognition.

Sacral Plexus
Orange and amber

This chakra is for procreation, sexuality, physical force and vitality. Here we find our emotions, desires, pleasure, sexual/ passionate love, change, assimilation of new ideas, health , family, surrender, giving and receiving and working harmoniously with others.

Glandular Connection: It relates to the lymphatic system.

Blockages: When this chakra is blocked we find over-indulgence in food and sex, sexual difficulties, confusion, jealousy, envy, desire to possess, impotence, lack of purpose, feeling of helplessness.

Root Chakra

Red and deep rose - the lowest vibrational rate

Here is our base, which is why this is called the root chakra. The root functions are those of survival, self-preservation, natural instincts, and vitality to the physical body, all matters relating to the material world. Everything relating to the physical world is found here - success, mastery of the body, stability, health, patience, security, courage and of course being grounded.

Glandular Connection: This chakra works with the gonads which relates to sexual functioning, fertility and instincts.

Blockages: Blocks in this chakra make us self-centered, tense, insecure, greedy, angry, overly concerned with one's physical survival, and sometimes violent.

As you read and understand the importance and function of each chakra and what happens when one is blocked in the energy flow, you can see how various responses in your own life develop as a result of these blockages. It is suggested by many people who work with energy fields that you remember the colors of each chakra and utilize that color in helping to remove and clear the blocks. Here is an example. You are feeling insecure. Your money is tight and you are worried about whether or not you can keep your house because there are rumors that you might lose your job. You feel angry over the situation. To help clear away potential blockages wear something red that day or maybe place a red lighted candle in your bathroom as you get ready for work. Perhaps you can buy yourself some red flowers and place them where you can see them. This can help you to re-focus your energy into positive patterns

and bring you back into a feeling of security, courage and patience as you ground yourself.

Note: the red color might be too strong and over-stimulating, so a deep rose or pink-red might be a better choice.

It was mentioned at the beginning of this section that the chakras can have *under* or *over* reactions. If there is an *over* reaction in the physical realm the softer shades of color should be used. When an *under* reaction is happening it is probably best to use a more vibrant shade of the color. It is advantageous to "stroke" the body with a very light touch and combine it with holding the hands over the chakra points or organs where blockages occur.

As you study these chakras you will notice that the top four primarily deal with spiritual awareness, the divine self, real love and connection with your Higher Power. People in this space can experience real love and share that with others. They are our inspired writers, speakers, artists, and healers who strive to help others in loving service. The bottom three chakras are more related to survival, money, sexuality, family, greed, pleasure and emotions, which are all more connected with the physical. Most people focus on these three energy areas most of their lives and operate from these charkas. This is where most people discover love as they think it is, coming from a purely physical place that we know doesn't remain the same. When individuals are in a survival mode, driven to find success and wealth, or are seeking relationships for neediness and desire, they are coming from these charkas primarily.

"The problems of this world cannot possibly be solved by skeptics or cynics whose horizons are limited by the obvious realities. We need men(women) who can dream of things that never were."

- John F. Kennedy, Former President of the United States

Review

1. Women have assumed the submissive role in a patriarchal society
*We have remained in this role from our old beliefs that
no longer serve our higher purpose.*

∞

2. Most of us have operated with low self-esteem all of our lives.
*This belief, according to psychologists, affects most of our society today.
As a result, we often attract relationships due to need.*

∞

3. There are two basic parts to our operating base:
the desire for love and the need to survive.

∞

4. Everything in the universe is composed of energy, including us.
*Energy is powerful and creates our life. Wherever we focus
our energy is where our power is.*

∞

5. Our system is composed of seven energy centers called chakras.
*Chakra means "wheel" which describes the spinning out effect of
energy from these centers. The chakras create wholeness within us.*

The seven chakras from head to toe are:

*Crown: Inspiration, Divine Oneness - Violet
Third Eye: Intuition, Clairvoyance, Spiritual Perception - Dark Blue
Throat: Communication, Writing, Arts, Speech - Shades of Blue
Heart: Love, Forgiveness, Compassion, Acceptance, Peace - Green
Solar Plexus: Emotions, Personal Power, Will - Yellow
Sacral Plexus: Procreation, Sexuality, Vitality - Orange
Root: Survival, Natural Instincts, Health, Success - Red*

Empowerment Activity

Identify two or more patterns of low self-esteem in you
that you continually repeat.

1. _____

2. _____

Indicate where these patterns fall in the chakras.

1. _____

2. _____

How can you shift those lower self images to higher self energy
that operates from the top four chakras.

1. _____

2. _____

Affirmation

*I choose love that operates from a spiritual
plane instead of the need of the world.*

Like a veil that
alters our perception,
the illusion of fear
blocks our imagination.

- Carolyn Porter

3
An Illusion

*F*alse Evidence Appearing Real. That is fear. Fear is something we imagine could happen but rarely does. It's something in the future but it affects us now, today, in our everyday lives. How can this be? How can we allow something that's an illusion of something not even real to create so many barriers in our lives? How can we allow this illusion to control our lives to the point of staying put when we should be moving forward, of cowering when we should stand tall, of hiding when we should be out in front leading the way, or turning our backs when we should confront and face whatever needs to be faced? It's simple. We are afraid. Afraid we aren't good enough, or capable enough, or smart enough, or deserving enough, or strong enough, or important enough, or attractive enough, or desired enough, or worthy enough, or loved enough. Fear places screens in front of our vision that block the reality of where we are. The screens, created by our ego, make us forget our divine power, the gifts already within us, and the unlimited possibilities in our life if we would only grab onto that power and knock down the screens.

Anything negative takes more energy to sustain, and this is the case with fear. When we hold onto the fear and keep it blocking the realness already within, we expend more energy to retain that negative pattern. Call it an energy waster! No wonder we wear ourselves out as we hang onto all our fears. The funny thing is that as we break through the fear and look back on it, it really was no big deal. We laugh and say "How silly of me" but then we go right back and do it again in another scene.

Let's take the fear of public speaking as an example since many say it's the number one fear in our society today. Here's the scenario. An individual has been coerced into speaking in front of a group of 25 people. This individual is so afraid that he hasn't been able to sleep well for days. It consumes his thoughts all through the day and he just wants to get it over and never commit to do something like this again. He finds his hands shaking for no reason other than the anticipation of standing in front of those 25 people. What is he afraid of? More than likely he's afraid he'll forget his talk, or that he'll look bad in front of important people, or perhaps he's afraid he'll stumble over his words or say something really dumb. Most likely he's thinking he's not good enough to do this and feels stupid for ever agreeing to do it. But the day finally comes, he gets up and presents his talk and everyone applauds his accomplishment. Now he can relax! And reflecting about all his worries he admits to himself that it wasn't as bad as he thought it would be. In fact, he's actually proud of himself, and he should be proud because *he did it!*

This man's fear stems from within himself, and it is a result of negative programming he's been taught that says he's not good enough. He feels defective and imperfect so he projects those thoughts from his sub-conscious into his conscious mind, which makes him a nervous wreck. I can understand this fear. I was so nervous when I went to my speaker's training that I was visibly shaking and so were my clothes. You should have felt my heart as I stood up the first time! But guess what, I did it, and I did it again, and now I do it all the time. What did I discover in the process of "doing it?" I found that when I went ahead and stood up and spoke, the fear went away, or at least most of it. I found that it wasn't as bad as my illusion had made it, and that the more I did it the easier it was. I found that all I was doing was sharing from my heart and that my purpose was not to be better than anyone, but to give something of value to those who were listening. I also learned that as I turned it over to God and asked for help, it came! It was never about me in the first place, it was about giving of myself to others and living my purpose.

Fear keeps us stuck. We get stuck in situations, relationships, beliefs, patterns and unhappiness because we are afraid to get out of our box and expand ourselves. We justify our sabotaging thoughts with self-talk such as "I don't have enough time," "Anyone is better than no one as a partner," "Maybe he'll change," " I can't do it," "I'm not strong enough," "I'm too tired," "My health isn't good enough," "I don't have enough resources," and so on. All these sabotaging thoughts are true because we believe they are true. We desperately cling to our model of the world. We forget where our source of power and possibilities are and we stay in fear of accomplishing what we really want to do. We want security and feeling comfortable, so we remain and dance the dance that allows our spirit to slowly die.

Here's another example of fear. Let's say you've been married twenty years. You've been unhappy for years but wanted to keep the family together. You stayed for all concerned, but particularly for the children. The children have grown up and are leaving home.

You're finding it difficult to enjoy much in life. There is little communication with your mate to the point that you often don't even speak to each other. You suspect he's been unfaithful a time or two. You know you should leave but don't like the feeling of getting into that uncomfortable place of the unknown. You repeatedly ask yourself "Where would I live?" "Would I be able to make enough money to support myself?" "Would my children be angry that I did this?" "What would other people say?" "Would I have to be alone the rest of my life?" "There really aren't any good men left our there." "Where would I fit in then?" "I would lose my 'couple' friends." "What would happen for holidays?" "I'd have to give up my house which I love. After all I put a lot of time and energy into this house." "I'd have to change my lifestyle and live more frugally."

And so this woman decides to remain, at least for now. She's afraid to move forward because she doubts her capabilities even though she knows inside she needs to detach from this negative relationship. Even though the pain is great by remaining, she still needs the security of knowing she's taken care of in a physical way. She is afraid of not surviving and in her confusion she operates from the blocked part of her root chakra, repressing once again her realness by giving her power to fear, and ultimately to those who represent this fear. The fear ensnares her as she places the screen in front of her thought processes and rationalizes them, thus allowing an illusion to block the reality of her being. This is a subtle manifestation of fear because all her questions are "normal" questions asked by most women in a similar situation. She has created her limited "box" for living.

I asked many of these questions as I was contemplating leaving my long marriage. In fact, I repeatedly asked these questions for years, always doubting whether I could make it on my own. I even thought that maybe, if I found someone else along the way, I could leave my present relationship and move right into another. What a disaster that would have been! If that had occurred, and many folks do this very thing, I would have attracted the same type of person and simply re-lived the same experience with a different face. There must be healing time and as I look back over the years since I left that relationship, I realize I am so completely different and have expanded into a new level of consciousness, that I cringe to think of what my life would be if I had proceeded into another relationship immediately. All those sabotaging thoughts of my incapabilities didn't materialize, so my fears were unwarranted after all. Sure, there were times when things seemed tough, but that was always when I slipped into the fear mode. I managed through everything I had to do because I made up my mind to do it. That's the secret - decide and do it! But always remember to surrender *your* will and watch God work miracles!

Because fear plays such a big role in the choices we make as women (men too), let's examine three of the most prevalent fears associated with detaching from a relationship that no longer serves. As a wholeness coach I have witnessed these fears in many women who are still hanging on to a relationship, whether personal or business, even when they know they shouldn't. In every one of these fears is the fear of failing which has been ingrained into our subconscious through eons of time.

Fear of Being Alone

By nature, most people prefer sharing life with someone else. Although some people enjoy being alone, most people don't. We are social beings and it is natural for an individual to seek out a partner. When a person is suddenly alone, perhaps for the first time, it can create a great deal of fear. Even if you've been alone

for years, there is usually a desire to find someone to share your life.

In the case of newly acquired aloneness, there can be fear due to lack of skills you haven't needed before. Perhaps you never had to manage the finances, insurance, income tax or things of this nature. Maybe you don't have a mechanical mind and are now faced with figuring out how to operate various items in your home. There can be the fear for your safety and of course silence can be deafening at times.

Another part of being alone is the fear of not being desired. It smashes our ego to think we are not desired emotionally and physically, so rejection and perhaps abandonment figures into the picture. We place so much validity in the physical connection that this aspect alone drives many folks into another relationship without healing time. If someone desires them physically they feel validated and special, but this is ego and ego thoughts are delusional.

I understand many of these fears through my own experience. I hated being alone but on the other hand I knew I must heal and grow in order to attract a different quality person into my life. But knowing it doesn't make it easy; that was certainly true for me. I also knew my healing would take time and there was no shortcut to the process. This is where so many people get into trouble. The process of growth is uncomfortable and somewhat painful until you realize how important it is and quit resisting, knowing it takes time.

I began asking questions and learning skills I didn't know I could learn. The key was in doing it and figuring it out along the way. Once the resistance is over, peace begins to flow and the sun seems to shine. Your attitude improves and things look brighter. You might even begin to enjoy your own company! I personally reached of point of being thankful for my freedom - freedom to do what I wanted and the freedom to grow.

So what is the solution to overcoming your fear of loneliness? First of all, tackle the things that are scariest first. Get help, ask questions, take classes, read and learn, whatever it takes to allow your own growth. Remember, there are no limitations to what you can do if you take away your self-imposed limitations. You are aware of the fear and you feel it, but you plow right through it with action. Once you're in the process of doing it, the fear vanishes. So you make a few mistakes along the way - you learn that way! Maybe it's time to be with yourself so you can understand exactly what you want your life to be. Walks, sitting in nature, meditating, prayer, reading, listening, all have immeasurable benefits for your expansion and growth. Maybe you will be taught patience and understanding as well as the power in "just being."

And here is the place that halts most individuals. They don't want to go inside and take a good look at what's there. They are afraid of what they might see. Change is hard for most people so they try to avoid it, but release and surrender is even harder. People want to control their lives. Letting go and getting out of the way so God can do the work is very difficult for most because it makes them feel helpless. However, once you can take your hands off miracles happen. The fear dissipates, the rainbow displays its beauty and the storm is over.

As you go through this process of accepting aloneness as okay while allowing yourself to expand past your previous beliefs, you must learn to love yourself. Since individuals commonly feel inadequate and undeserving of good, they often find it difficult to love themselves. How can you ever love another human being if you don't love yourself? It isn't possible. Love is a state of being and it is not outside of you but comes from deep within you. It all begins with you and as you recognize this you'll understand more fully the power in being alone, at least for a while. When I could finally honestly say that I love myself just as I am, that I appreciate

who I am and what my place is in the world, that I knew there were no limitations to the abundance in my life now and in the future, I realized the miracle of me. It's when I surrendered my life for service that I knew I had broken through the barrier of fear and become love, for love is all there is.

There's another kind of aloneness, the aloneness within a relationship. So many people live separate lives within the relationship because they are too afraid to leave it and be themselves. I have seen this with my clients, friends and even family members. Some people actually have their rooms on different floors because they don't want to be in each other's company. One couple I know, in their 70's, live this way because they feel at their age there is no other choice. When they are in each other's presence there is apparently a lot of bickering and unpleasantness. Another woman who was a customer in my health store when I was actively running the store, said that she was too old to make changes in her life (she was 56 at the time) and had resigned herself to an empty life. Her comment was that it was too much trouble to start again. What a way to live! Their spirits were dying and they accepted it. In fact, these examples of unhappy relationships impacted me to the point of realizing this wasn't the way I wanted to live my life. To me it was like giving up and giving in, and that just wouldn't work for me. There was no way I was going to live the rest of my life under the negative influence I was experiencing and end up like those relationships. These insights forced me out of my box into the unknown which eventually brought me freedom to be the person I am meant to be.

When you live in fear you cannot live from love, for these two emotions cannot exist simultaneously. They are opposing energies. All love is the love of God, so if you are in fear you are not in alignment with God. But allow the love in and you are never alone, never! It's up to you. You can choose fear…or love?

Fear of Financial Instability

This is a tough area to address because in most cases, people find the financial strain of being alone one of the biggest challenges. This is especially true for a woman. Women generally find high-paying jobs scarce for them, and although times have changed and are continually changing, it is a known fact that it is still much more difficult for a woman to earn high wages than it is for a man. If there are children involved it becomes even more challenging.

We live in a physical world. We have responsibilities and yet we want to enjoy life without financial struggle. Life isn't meant to be a struggle but most of us have been taught it is. And so that's the life we create - one of struggle, lack and disenchantment. Worst of all is the fact that we accept it as the way it is meant to be.

The first thing we must do, regardless of where we are financially, is decide we want our finances stable and put a clear vision in our mind of what we want, even to naming an amount we expect to make monthly or yearly. This is called intention and here's how it works. You begin with gratitude for what you already have. This is very important. Then you state your intention to the universe of what you see for yourself in the way of prosperity for you - envisioning your desires. It must always be for the highest and best for you and others. Don't expect miracles if you only ask for lots of money so you can live affluently; that would be coming from ego and operating negatively from the lower chakras in the physical realm. Instead, think of ways to use your abundance that help you and others in expanding past where you presently are. This approach always involves spirit which means you are coming from a place of love - the top four charkas that include the heart and divine oneness.

As you envision your life without the struggle of finances, focus on everything you can picture with much emotion, for the emotion

is what makes it happen. Consider your thoughts. A thought is just a thought, but if you attach emotion to that thought it changes completely. It becomes real, and it is the realness of the vision that turns it into reality. Remember it's all energy and energy creates. It sounds simple doesn't it? In reality it is because the universe is abundant and there is more than enough for everyone on this planet to live a life of prosperity without the struggle. So what happens that the abundance seems to elude us?

Fear! The fear pops in with self-sabotaging thoughts of failure, lack, rejection, aloneness, and struggle. And the fear comes into our consciousness due to our own thoughts. Even if we listen to other people and they help us with our doubts, it is ultimately our own choice that places us in the "Life is a Struggle" mindset.

We live in a world that demands we pay our bills and pay them on time. That's our reality, so let's see how to make our reality fun and rewarding. Maybe you have a job you hate but must stay there to pay the bills. Maybe you lost your job and you must move into something new - your reason for the fear at this time. Perhaps your job doesn't pay enough for your new state of aloneness and you're having trouble making ends meet. You are afraid of failing.

Faith is the answer, faith that God will sustain you and bring you what you need. This concept is difficult for so many people. Why? Because faith involves trusting something not seen, and we want facts, something we can see. Believing that God will come through with a plan when you see the bills piling up and you don't know which way to turn takes faith. But it also takes action. God gave us unlimited intelligence and we must use it. God expects us to be diligent with our gifts and use the brainpower and discernment we have to utilize the opportunities that are given us. Here's how it works.

You have a challenge that seemingly has no way out. So you pray to God acknowledging that you are surrendering this problem, letting go of the situation, and that you are willing to do whatever is necessary to remedy this situation. Then you release it, knowing God will bring an answer. Maybe it'll mean you need to get a second job and an opportunity will suddenly show up. Perhaps a promotion will amazingly appear in the job you already have. Maybe a new person will unexpectedly cross your path with new possibilities, or maybe that relationship that has been so difficult will heal. Whatever you need will show up in some form if you believe it will. It means keeping a smile on your face and a song in your heart because you know that your Creator, who is part of you, is taking care of you.

Let's examine an example of this process so you can understand how to make your life change its reality. There are five steps to this process.

Your first step is the *Desire* to make your life happen. You look at your monthly expenses. You see that you need $3000 per month to pay your present bills. This includes all expenses except things like vacations or trips and the unexpected that appears from time to time. You want to save for emergencies as well as do some investing for your future. So you decide that $6000 per month is what you need to make your life what you currently want. (Understand that you can change your expectations any time you want!)

Decision is your second step. Begin by stating your intention to the universe. In so doing, you are saying that you have made a decision to move forward with this plan and are willing to do whatever it takes to follow through with it. You always have a choice, but if you commit to doing something, then you must do it. State your intention that you desire $6000 per month so you can enjoy life more as you pay your bills and become financially independent. State that this makes you feel powerful and helps you to empower others too. Mention the good things that can

happen as you are free to enjoy life instead of struggling as you've done in the past. State it as if it is already done, with a thankful heart.

Envision yourself living a life with $6000 per month income. What are you wearing or what type of house do you live in? Picture it in detail using all your senses. What colors do you see around you, what does your house look like? How do you act when you're feeling good and enjoying that $6000 per month? What do you smell? How do you feel? How is it benefiting others? Once you have the vision you must keep it alive daily. *Envisioning* is the third step. Do this daily for the more you see it the more you believe it. "Feeling" the picture makes it more realistic, believing it will come to pass.

Belief is the fourth step and where so many of us fall short. We know it in our head perhaps, but actually doubt that it can happen. We project out this fear and doubt which in turn keeps the abundance from reaching us, even though it's right on the other side of the doubt. Belief and doubt are conflicting energies so they bump heads. Then we say it doesn't work when we are the ones who got in our own way. Belief involves allowing God to take over as we surrender our will. Belief means we let go of the "how" because we believe that God knows the situation better than we do and can work out the details so much easier.

This is the *Knowing*, the knowing that with God all things are possible. This fifth step means that even though we can't imagine how it will work out for us, we are trusting God's divine power to work a miracle. The knowing gives us great peace and joy and replaces the worry, which is simply a form of fear. Then when the answer suddenly appears, we just smile and say "Thank you!"

The Fear of Rejection

Rejection is a very negative emotional response. A person who feels rejected feels like a discard or worthless, and probably betrayed. This might apply particularly to a woman whose partner left the relationship to be with a different woman. But it can apply to anyone in a relationship that disintegrates, regardless of which "side" you are on. Rejection feeds the ego because it feeds the victim mindset. Rejection also buys into the low self-esteem most people have already adopted as a mainstay belief pattern.

There are several aspects to the theme of rejection. One is the rejection as a woman in the physical realm. We have placed such emphasis on attracting the male that the thought that a man doesn't find us desirable any more can be devastating for many women. This goes right back to the low self-worth that's been the way of life for an individual up to then, but if a hard look is taken at this response it indicates the "neediness" that is present. Worth and desirability have been based on this one person, and she is letting this man control her by her response.

This is a normal feeling, and it's okay to feel the hurt initially, but so many women don't "get it" and they immediately seek out another companion in order to feel desired. It may make them feel better about themselves for a while, but it doesn't last because the core issue hasn't been resolved. No matter how many relationships this woman enters into, she will never be happy or feel her own worth if she bases it on her physical desirability by a man. Don't get me wrong; it is wonderful to be desired by a partner as an addition to your life, as long as your value isn't based on being desired by that person or anyone else.

Another aspect of rejection is social rejection or the loss of "couple" activities. The social lives of many women are created around activities with other couples. When a relationship ends so ends the couple activities and therefore ends the social life. Usually, even with great friendships, it is never the same again and the friendships fade away. This person lost her partner and then the friends that went with the relationship. So it feels like another rejection through the mistaken perception in her mind.

Without realizing it, the woman feels unworthy inside, perhaps breeding shame, guilt, resentment and maybe even anger that things had to change. On top of that is the loss of the friendships, but even more is the loss of identity. She was part of the relationship of this group, this neighborhood, and now they are all gone. Where does she fit? This is tough for most people and starting again is not easy. But this is how life is, ever-changing. Now you build new friendships and "find" who you are in this aloneness state.

Sometimes when there are children involved there can be challenges that signal rejection from the children. Maybe they seem to blame you for this state of affairs or perhaps they are torn between the two parents and seem to reject you. There might be antagonism from your former partner so that it appears he has manipulated the children to "his side." Perhaps even family members are disappointed or upset and send those energies to you in the form of rejection. So you take it all upon yourself and feel very guilty, wondering if you made a mistake but knowing deep inside that you didn't. You're confused and feeling guilty which allows a heyday for your ego as you sink lower and lower into self-doubt, low self-esteem and possibly depression.

But the deepest manifestation of rejection often comes from within your own being. You don't really understand it, but you have grabbed onto the vibrations sent from other people and have made them your own. You bury them deep inside so that you actually feel less and less important, less valuable and ultimately not worthy of anything good. At this point you are rejecting the good things in life because you have rejected your own goodness.

This creates a rather dismal picture of a life not worth living because you have basically rejected the goodness of God. When you reject God's goodness you are actually rejecting yourself, for you are one with God.

Although there are many forms of fear that enter our lives on a daily basis, we have addressed three that seem to be present in almost everybody's life at one point, whether alone or in a relationship. Sometimes, even with a partner, these fears can be evident.

But since fear is an illusion, something not even real, how can we allow it to rule our lives? Why not take the fear apart and shift our thoughts to love, for love is the opposite of fear. There are only two real emotions - fear or love. Fear produces contracting negative feelings such as hate, jealousy, hurt, resentment, bitterness, anger, shame, guilt, victim, rage, spitefulness, despair, judgment, weakness and so on. Love gives us expanding positive feelings that include compassion, appreciation, kindness, strength, power, hopefulness, gratitude, peace, faith, trust, humility, mercy, happiness and so on. Which would you prefer in your life, the illusion of fear or the realness of love?

Why not take each of these fears we discussed and make them into an exciting adventure? So you're alone. Change your perception and look at it this way. Now you don't have to answer to anyone, you can do what you want, when you want and how you want. You can decide to go out once a week or more and do something with other people, maybe go to new places and cultivate new friends, which is expansion. Perhaps now is the time to take those classes you always wanted to take, learn how to operate a computer or start learning the stock market. Imagine all the wonderful new people coming into your life and then watch them materialize from your own creation. Be thankful for the lessons you have learned and feel your own growth and strength. After

all, you made it this far. Invite friends over. Go out and enjoy life. It will be what you make it. Maybe it's time to be quiet for a while, which is the hardest thing I had to do. Or maybe it's time to start that business or a new career. The possibilities are endless if you just allow them in. But most of all find yourself. Open up to your realness and become the powerful being you already are.

Financial stability happens when you make a plan and implement it. It's really as simple as that. Maybe you need to find a reputable financial advisor or a coach to assist you, or perhaps you need to study and learn things for yourself. Look at this as an exciting adventure as well, for now you are grabbing your own power and taking steps to improve your life. Maybe it's time for you to show the world what you're made of. All you need do is let go of the fear and the control and allow God to do the rest. Miracles always happen to those who believe!

Here's another way to view rejection. Rejection is Protection! I heard Alan Cohen make this statement and it hit me about the validity of those words. Stop and think about circumstances that have come and gone in which you felt rejected, left behind, overlooked, or hurt. You moved past the circumstance, and looking back, realized what a blessing the rejection was. Perhaps you lost your job and although you dipped into the depths of fear for a while you now have acquired a new job that's so much better than the one before. So you say "Thank you God." Be grateful that you were protected from being part of a situation or relationship that was no longer for your highest good.

The negative feelings of rejection aren't easy to erase, but once you do it is so very freeing. You might need assistance from healers and people who specialize in release techniques. Read, study, meditate, pray and seek professional help if necessary. Surrender your thoughts and feelings and ask for divine help - it always works! It makes you take control of your thoughts, changing the negative ones to positive ones. Only you can do this and it does take time, so don't give up or get frustrated. You are worthy because you are part of God, and therefore, incredibly wonderful. Affirm this to yourself and learn to love yourself, for you are all you have.

This is a process that requires putting one foot in front of the other, one step at a time. Sometimes you'll stumble and may fall. That's okay. It happens to everyone. Get up, brush yourself off and take a quick inventory. Are you okay? Wipe away the tears and exchange them for a smile. Know this is a *gift*, a gift because you are growing and getting stronger with every step you take. You can't go back to where you were, and why would you want to? So look out over the horizon at the beautiful light that illumines your path, realizing you are on your way and will get there if you just keep placing one foot in front of the other.

As we leave this chapter on the illusion of fear, I want to make sure you understand the process of letting go of fear. Fear is amazingly deceptive in our lives and affects us in a magnanimous way, so I'm giving you a system to walk through the fear and heal.

Burn the fear and change it to ashes:

1. Become aware of it.

Recognize the fear and see it for what it is. Attach no judgment to it; simply see it.

2. Feel it.

Feel all the pain, hurt, embarrassment, resentment, anger, victimizing of it. You must experience the pain to be free of it. We couldn't understand day if there was no night.

3. Accept it as is.

You're aware of it, you've felt it and now you accept it. Okay, so I feel fear. Good. I know what it is. We're on our way!

4. Surrender it.

Letting go is the only way to be free of it. It's only an illusion so it cannot really block us unless we allow it to.

5. Move through it.

This is the part where you do it anyway! You break right through the unrealness of fear and experience exhilarating freedom.

"You gain strength, courage and confidence by every experience in which you really stop to look fear in the face…You must do the thing you think you cannot do."

- Eleanor Roosevelt, Former First Lady

Review

1. Fear is an illusion that often controls our real lives.
*We are afraid that we aren't good enough so we can't accomplish
what we might want to do. Fear is something we imagine but rarely
ever happens. Fear keeps us stuck in relationships, patterns, beliefs,
situations and unhappiness.*

✍

2. Leaving a relationship can be difficult for many people to do.
The reasons are:

a. Fear of Being Alone
*We are faced with learning new skills, handling finances, creating
enough income and being alone. People often seek another
relationship to fill the void within themselves. They are
afraid of knowing themselves.*

b. Fear of Financial Instability
*This fear is one of the big ones because women may not be able
to make equal salary to men. It is necessary to create a plan and
envision what you want. The five steps to making your life happen
are: Desire, Decision, Envision, Belief and Knowing.*

c. Fear of Rejection
*A woman who has been rejected feels undesirable and worthless.
Many things change when a relationship disengages, including
friendships, especially if the partner found someone else.*

✍

3. Burning the fear - 5 steps.

Empowerment Activity

Breaking through the illusion of fear would allow me to:

1. _____

2. _____

3. _____

4. _____

5. _____

6. _____

7. _____

8. _____

Imagine how wounderful this life would be!

Affirmation

*I choose to move forward in love and break
through the limiting illusion of fear.*

Pushing against the flow of life
will eventually destroy your life.

- Carolyn Porter

4

Resistance

*M*ost of us are experts in resistance. Resistance is the act of opposition, or working against something. Resistance is telling God we don't like the way things are and we want it to look different! We might even "fight" to keep the control. Resistance guarantees that judgment, blame, victim and non-acceptance are involved - all derivatives of fear - and the resistance makes life seem difficult if not unbearable.

Another explanation for resistance is causing electricity to be transformed into heat. Think of it in terms of energy. We want it our way. We get upset or angry for the turn of events in our life. We focus our attention on this negative energy so that's where our power is. Energy causes things to happen. Energy creates heat, and if it's negative we might experience the emotions of anger, frustration, resentment, bitterness, close-mindedness - all branches of fear. On the other hand, if we send that energy with positive force, we

51

experience the warmth of love expressed as compassion, caring, gratitude, kindness, genuineness, forgiveness and openness. Each experience in which we concentrate our power through energy creates a form of either fear or love.

We've already discussed that we are one with God and that God is love. If God is love would He allow us challenges that aren't good for us? Here we must open up to faith, for faith and love are synonymous. But we believe we have all the answers so we get in the way of our own progress. We think we know exactly what we need in our life, so we resist what enters our path. Let's look at some examples of life expressing as resistance.

Perhaps there's been a constant urging inside you to move into a different work scenario. You know you're better qualified for a particular position and you deserve the opportunity to show your expertise, and you certainly know you deserve the increase in income. But the boss keeps promoting someone else instead. It's happened three times in the last year. In addition, new guidelines have been incorporated into the company and you're not able to do all the creative things you were doing. You are frustrated and even angry. You're having trouble sleeping because you feel great injustice over this situation. It's beginning to affect the work you were doing so well before and you are feeling quite unhappy. You've thought about starting your own business but are afraid you can't do it. You are resisting the situation with emotional negativity because you have decided how it is supposed to look.

So what are your options? The resisting is getting you nowhere. If you remain where you are your work will probably just continue to go downhill and then you could lose your job. So why not quit resisting and surrender? Surrender isn't easy for most people because we are controllers and we want things the way we want them when we want them, and that is that. Then we wonder why we get ourselves into so many situations that create such negative results in our life. Here are some choices you could make. First, you must surrender the situation and let God take over. Once you have achieved true surrender - getting totally out of the way and accepting that you don't know best - you can acknowledge the fact that you must make some changes in order to achieve what you desire. You could discuss with your employer what it is that is necessary for you to be promoted. Or perhaps you must sit quietly and accept where you are until Divine Guidance comes through loud and clear. Could this be a signaling for you to move out by yourself and create something wonderful from within you? Are things difficult at your job because you're not supposed to be there anymore? Are you resisting change, growth and expansion instead of experiencing unlimited possibilities?

When we surrender any situation and get out of our own way, thus allowing God to work out the details, miracles happen. I cannot remember one situation in my life that I was trying to run my way that didn't resolve easily and perfectly once I let go of it entirely. The end result was much better than anything I could have imagined. We are control freaks, resisting over and over again, afraid to relinquish the control and become powerless. The ironic part of it all is that when we yield to God's will we actually gain our power and are able to become masters. Surrendering means submitting our will which places us in total alignment for the right and perfect solution. Surrendering means to understand the profound wisdom of yielding instead of our resisting to the flow of life. *Surrendering means we give up to God our perception of all things!* In the frustrating job situation just mentioned, if this person surrenders her will and allows the situation to heal, either the job will open up new possibilities, the individual will change her perception of the whole situation, or new doors will open for this individual to move in a more creative venture that serves the highest and best for all. So whatever the solution is, this person is a winner.

Too often we scream and kick and try to fight God because we don't trust. Have you ever attempted to take a splinter out of a child's finger who is resisting the process but who is hurting and crying and wants it out? This circumstance was cited in *Beyond Codependency* by Melody Beattie. "One day my daughter got a sliver in her finger. It really hurt and I had to take it out. But taking it out hurt too. I held my daughter on my lap. I talked softly to her. I tried to be gentle. But she kicked, screamed, and fought all the way. I tried to tell her that if she relaxed and stopped fighting it wouldn't hurt so much. I tried to tell her if she just trusted me the pain would be gone before she knew it. But she was too scared to trust. When I got the sliver out, she was so mad she just cried and beat on my arms. It hurt that she didn't trust me. It hurt more that she had made her pain worse than it had to be."

How many of us have done the same thing? Maybe you? Maybe me? We are so mad at God for our situation and resist with such force that we make our pain even greater. And that hurts God because God only wants us to trust that all the hurts in our life can be removed if we relax and let go. By fighting we make the pain greater and it often lasts longer.

Another example is when a relationship falls apart. Your boyfriend has found someone new to replace you and has been seeing this person behind your back. You are hurt and feel rejected and abandoned. You feel great anger and don't understand how this guy could do this to you. You thought you had such a great relationship with many common interests and plans for the future. But suddenly it changes and you can't accept it. Your anger is never released and you turn it inside. Your ego is damaged and you have relinquished your identity by emotionally attaching to this relationship as you want it to be. Without realizing what you are doing you act from unresolved anger, and create another relationship with someone else, allowing it to escalate into a commitment. You have a new man and you think you're happy, but you created the relationship solely to spite your old boyfriend. It's all a result of your subconscious negative thought process being justified by your ego. But as time goes by you realize you're actually unhappy and eventually become quite miserable. You blame your partner for your unhappiness and go deeper into depression. You lose interest in your personal appearance and in life itself, and pull back from the world with all kinds of emotional and physical problems. Years have gone by and your life becomes a "going through the motions" existence. This is a true story of one couple I know, but also depicts the story of many other relationships.

What happened in this story is an example of resistance to the fact that it was time to let go of the relationship, no matter how painful, and surrender it for the highest and best for all. Because the anger was never released and the situation never surrendered, this person allowed her previous partner to control her life and keep her in a very stuck place. She reacted by creating a miserable life based on unresolved anger and resistance. When we fight against our highest and best, we always lose. She was stuck in her own bondage, a prisoner of her own creation, but never saw the light beyond the darkness.

Here's another example of resistance to the process of life. A woman had three children who have been the main focus of her life. They brought her much happiness and busyness and helped her hide from her own self. They grew up and left the nest and suddenly she's lost. What does she do now? She gets a job, a mindless job to occupy her time. But she keeps her hands in her children's lives with daily phone calls, giving her opinions as to how they should be living, voicing her opinion over their finances, relationships, spending, activities, or whatever else comes to her mind, without being asked. Her life is still evolving around her children. She is trying to control their lives in order to fill up the void their leaving has created in her. The children love her but are tired of her interference. They've grown up and want to experience their own path with or without her approval. That is how it should be, but this woman is resisting the natural progression of life. So they begin pulling away, trying to avoid her confrontations and opinions by not answering their phone or not returning her calls. They make excuses for not meeting her or stopping by to visit. And then they feel guilty for allowing themselves the privilege of living their own lives even though it is their birthright. So a cycle of control through manipulation of emotions has developed because of the basic issue of resistance to the natural rhythm of the cycle of life.

Once again we see that resistance manifested as unhappy situations such as this, and that it could eventually destroy the relationship this woman has with her children. Children have a birthright to walk their own path. No parent can live the child's life nor should they attempt to do so, for it will constrict the child's growth. Letting go can be difficult if you don't realize why or understand the benefits of doing so. The benefits are for the growth of that child, who really is a spirit on loan to you and is a great teacher as well for a few short years. Letting go of your children also benefits your own growth. You cannot proceed on your journey if you're always trying to walk another's path. Not only will it never work, but it keeps you from opening to your own greatness that's waiting to illumine the world. Ironically, by trying to control their lives you have allowed these people to control yours.

Reflection on Resistance

Looking back at these three examples of resistance, there are some things common to each situation. Pain is in the physical reality of life, whether it is emotional, mental or physical. Pain signifies thoughts - our mind in action - creating these undesirable manifestations of the resistance in fear. When we resist we bring unnecessary pain into our lives and it locks us in the experience. Debbie Ford states in her book *The Secret of the Shadow* "Resistance locks us inside the emotional pain of the situation." But we are also in the state of competition. Let's look at each story again and see the comparables of pain and competition.

In the first story the woman was in competition for her "right" to a promotion. She didn't receive her desire so she felt the pain of her ego thoughts that she didn't get what she perceived she deserved. Her body reacted with anger which turned into insomnia and created negative circumstances in her physical existence that came from fear, which we now know is an illusion. What a different outcome there would have been if she had only acknowledged her desire for the promotion and that she felt she deserved it, but then surrendered the outcome to her Creator. She had a choice. She could have experienced peacefulness instead of worry and frustration, and undoubtedly would have gone right to sleep because she knew who was handling her desires and outcome.

The second story exhibits the same patterns of pain and competition. The woman feels the pain of rejection and abandonment, and simultaneously she feels competition with another woman who took her place. Her emotional identity was with the boyfriend through the powerlessness of codependence, and it was so strong that she married someone else just to "spite" the boyfriend. We see how it backfired for her as she found herself in an unhappy life experience from the ego-induced negative emotions that arose from the effects of losing her boyfriend. As it was in the case of the first story, this person was operating from blockages in the lower three chakras, creating jealousy, the demand for power and success, lack of purpose, helplessness and insecurities.

Even through the third story we again see the pattern of pain and competition. The mother who was attempting to control the lives of her children felt great pain as they left the nest. They had been her life and she felt empty. It's a natural phenomenon for any mother to feel some emptiness as the children leave, but this woman exemplified an emotional codependence that was totally unhealthy and unnatural. It caused her great emotional pain as she felt the negative of competition from the fact that they wanted to live their own lives instead of through her. She was competing with their individuality and independence.

In all of these previously mentioned life encounters there is pain and competition, and where there is pain and competition there is *Control Hunger*. *Control Hunger* is our ego's way of telling us we have to be in the driver's seat or we won't have what we want in life. The crafty ego manipulates our thoughts into the belief that pain is necessary and part of life, and that we have the "right" to feel this way. But pain and competition are not adjuncts of love, so we again see fear at the root of these difficult manifestations in our lives. Our ego thrives on fear and fear promotes the ego. What a pair!

Surrender has been mentioned several times, so let's make sure we understand exactly what surrender is. Surrender doesn't mean giving up and losing. Surrender means accepting the circumstances. It means voluntarily yielding to what is. It no longer judges the circumstance as negative, but instead simply allows the individual to remain unaffected by the temporary life situation that occurs. In no way does this mean to sit back and do nothing, but it does mean to eliminate the negative emotions. Surrender and action are totally compatible.

Here's an example of surrender with action. You are driving down the highway and your tire suddenly decides to lose all its air. You pull over to get out of the line of traffic, and then you have a choice. You can sit there on the side of the highway resigning yourself to a flat tire and accepting this undesirable situation, or you can use your cell phone to call your road service or possibly hail someone driving by to stop and help you. If you choose the first option, you have not really surrendered. You've resigned yourself to what has happened and allowed yourself to become a victim. The other two choices involve action. You surrender to the situation by accepting the circumstance of a flat tire, and you yield to the process of what needs to occur to fix the tire. Resigning to a life situation is really becoming a victim. Surrendering to the life experience is a positive consciousness, knowing that it's there as a strength-builder. The ego deceives us in believing that resistance makes us stronger, but actually resistance produces weakness. If you think about the stories we've been discussing, you'll see the weakness that emerged in each individual as they allowed resistance to take over their focus.

Power of Our Mind in Resistance

Whenever we are experiencing resistance to our life situations, we are using the mind. The mind is ego, and when ego takes control of the situation, we have misrepresentation of the realness of life because we react to the circumstance. Reaction goes hand in hand with resistance and always signals ego at work. Surrender however, allows spirit to work by bringing spiritual energy into the situation. Spirit at work reconnects us to our Oneness and the Source of all power. When this happens, we see things through different eyes. There's a positive force that allows the flow of life from love. The action taken through surrendering the circumstance perpetuates a new consciousness of peacefulness and acceptance which comes from alignment to that love. We become very real. Life is simple and we are vulnerable. The vulnerability allows us to throw away

the defensiveness and masquerade of resistance that hides the realness of ourselves.

The ego is a masterful force field that thrives in the caverns of fear. Ego propels us away from love and seeks to control our mental functions. It works similar to an autoimmune disease which attacks a person's own body, as ego uses our mind consciousness and attacks our spirit self. Anytime we choose judgment, resistance, control, selfishness or greed we are opening our arms to the wiles of our ego. And is it clever, convincing us that we must protect ourselves from the injustices that people bestow upon us. The ego fights to survive, repeatedly telling us how unworthy we are and how we must fight for our rights to be in control. It tells us that if we don't control we lose and become weak, but the reality is that only through the power of surrender and love can we ever become the enlightened divine being with unlimited possibilities, a being who radiates from within pure love and shines loving, healing energy around the world.

We want peace in our lives, but as long as we resist and react there is no peace. We are hurt and we feel justified in harboring those feelings. That individual had no right to do what they did to us we think. But that state isn't a powerful, loving state of being. Marianne Williamson says, "If you can state, despite your resistance, your willingness to see the spiritual innocence, the light in the soul of one who has harmed you, you have begun the journey to a deep and unshakable peace." So we see the power that the mind holds for the direction of our relationships and our life experiences.

When we focus on resistance, or anything negative, that negative energy expands. Our thoughts are energy and create our life experience. If we are focusing on the undesirable occurrences, we expand those into bigger negative experiences, all of which are fear-based. We know that fear is an illusion so we are expanding the illusion. The life circumstances that our own energy is manifesting through our fear-driven thoughts, is an illusion! That's kind of scary isn't it? Here we are on this planet, spiritual beings having a human experience, an experience that is an illusion because we've forgotten who we really are. We are placing so much energy into this experience and delude ourselves into believing this is what we want. But our essence, which is of love, screams out to be reunited with that pure love from whence we came. We are in a delusional state whenever we allow the world's interpretation of love to surface into our consciousness and override the love within us. Every circumstance that takes away from our core awareness of love is a byproduct of illusion, or fear.

We are here to discover our realness. Realness is born only from love. Resistance is born of fear and cannot exist in the same space as love. When we accept what is without any reservations whatsoever, we have surrendered into God's unconditional love and power. The circumstance is not transformed. We are transformed. Wherever we focus our attention, there is the creation of our life experience. Come back to love and know the serenity of realness.

Resisting Change

In all of the examples I've shared thus far in this chapter, the element of change was portrayed. People as a rule don't like change. We get so complacent in our "box" because it feels comfortable and secure and we don't want to move. Change is something we experience throughout our lives; it is inevitable. We can resist it or flow with it. Our response to the change is of utmost importance to what happens thereafter. Without change, there can be no growth. When we resist change it is simply hardening of the attitudes!

You've probably experienced the rapid growth of a child in their first year of life. But what if this child didn't continue to grow at the expected rate? You would be alarmed and begin checking into why as soon as you suspected anything amiss. But the cycle of life continues and the child becomes an adolescent, then a teenager. Before you know it he's an adult starting his own family. The cycle of life continues. But isn't it just as important, if not more so, that we also grow in the dimensions other than physical? Oftentimes we pay no attention to these forgotten areas of growth.

Everyone gets those "gut" feelings. Maybe we feel inside that a change would be good for us but it's too frightening for us to move. Do we need to detach from that non-nurturing relationship? Is that job or profession of no interest to us anymore? Do we know we're being given divine guidance but are ignoring those nudgings? As a society we are often chasing our tails so to speak. We run in this direction and that direction feeling very scattered with all our duties to fulfill. We lose the enthusiasm of life for all its responsibilities and activeness. The eternal movement is so continuous that we never have time to think of anything other than the physical realm. We have lost our soul in the name of busyness. Busyness makes us look good in the eyes of the world, and maybe it deludes us into feeling better about ourselves. But this busyness actually keeps us in a state of mindlessness that perpetuates sameness and prevents growth.

I'm not talking about changes in external activities; I am talking about the change within. This change or this growth is of the spirit and has nothing to do with busyness. It's all about becoming the person we came into this lifetime to be. I'm talking about the shift in our conscious behavior that advances us into new dimensions of spirit and love that we are here to remember. It's not something we must learn for we knew it before and are simply remembering. But the only way we can move into the expansiveness of the universe is to become a dynamic person who invites the realm of the unknown into their reality.

No one is coming to rescue us. There is no knight on a white horse or a prince to kiss and wake us from our sleep. We have to do it all by ourselves, and it means taking the time to reach inside for the answers. Nothing on the outside can fix us. As long as we remain in resistance we exchange growth for stagnation. The tighter we hold on, the more energy we expend as we sink deeper into spiritual death.

We will be discussing how to get out of our "box" of sameness in pages to come, but understand that the principle of change means becoming. It is a gift! As the child needs to change in order to grow up to be an adult, so does each spirit need to change to grow into the beautiful expanded being that is our divine heritage to become. It is in this space that we are real and understand, perhaps for the first time in our life, the realness of who we are.

"In the end, it's not the years in your life that count; it's the life in your years."

- Abraham Lincoln, Former President of the United States

Review

1. Resistance means we are in the act of opposition.
We want things our way and when they don't go as we had planned, we often oppose the outcome.Allowing God to take over is a much better option.

✍

2. Surrender is the best way to go.
Relinquishing control is hard for most people, but it is how we come into love instead of fear. Surrender allows the good to come in. It may mean giving up a relationship that doesn't serve your highest and best any longer.

✍

3. Resistance brings pain and competition.
In the three stories shared there was evidence of pain and competition. This is a byproduct of our ego.

✍

4. Our mind is where the fear begins and creates the controlling resistance.
Our mind is powerful and is ruled by our ego. When we choose judgment, resistance, control, selfishness or greed we are living through the eyes of our ego. This is all illusion. If we change our thoughts to loving thoughts, we become real.

✍

5. Many times we resist change.
By nature many people want things to remain the same. As a result they don't wish to look within themselves and see what needs to shift. So they remain as they are, stuck in their own box.

Empowerment Activity

Identify situations you are resisting.

1. _____
2. _____
3. _____
4. _____

How would you feel if you let them go?

1. _____
2. _____
3. _____
4. _____

How could letting go and allowing God change your life?

_____
_____
_____

Affirmation

I choose to surrender all that I'm resisting and allow the flow of good to me that I deserve.

Our identity comes not
from wordly attachments,
but the light that shines
through our spirit - our truth.

- *Carolyn Porter*

5

Attachment

*H*ave you ever given thought to what an attachment is? You send an email to someone and add an attachment to that message. It simply means adding on, joining the original or connecting to it. When people connect in a relationship, your first thought might be that it is simply a connection, a good thing because you want to be with that person. But let's look deeper into the actual definition of attachment.

When individuals join together in a relationship, whether as friends or lovers, they feel connected to each other. The connection in a relationship is very important to us and is what draws us to that person to begin with. We could call it attraction or the "chemistry" necessary for the relationship.

But then we get confused. We begin feeling attached to that person. Attachment is a form of codependency or neediness that most individuals call love. This attachment

69

or codependency gives a sense of security that often becomes an emotional possessiveness. It imposes demands and asks for conformity to our desires. The codependency is based from fear which is propagated because of the ego, which means that the relationship is formed of neediness and therefore is an expansion of the ego. Ego is not of love. This relationship becomes multidimensional bondage and renders you powerless!

The world's view of love is really need. Need is a void within an individual that can only be filled from within, but we often look to another person to fill that need. We all have our own perceptions and expectations of what the other person should or shouldn't do, and those demands can become bondage. Both people are looking to the other for negating the insecurities and fears within themselves and they cannot understand why they aren't being resolved. Both are clinging to each other for validation of their worth and that clinginess is demonstrated in many ways.

While there is definitely a feeling of "completeness" in a marriage or partnership from the physical standpoint, the completeness of each partner in the spiritual and emotional realms must be from within. Although each partner can add much support to the growth and ultimate healing of that individual, the real inner work comes only from the soul of the partner who is growing. *When both partners give the other the freedom to grow and be who they are, the relationship is actually showing nonattachment.*

A person who is needy will attract another needy person and each will be trying to control the other. That is the definition of codependency - allowing someone else's behavior to affect you and control your life because you are obsessed with controlling that person's life. It's all about control. Partners wish to control each other by demanding certain actions according to their perceptions. Neither partner can be who they really are because they must always be thinking of how to get what they want from the relationship.

Neither one realizes this "manipulation" is going on because they're committed to the relationship, and they just assume that problems and misunderstandings are part of the relationship.

Here is an example of control in a "loving" relationship. The man keeps control of the finances, making it necessary for the woman to always ask for money for her expenses. Perhaps she has her own account into which he deposits money regularly, requiring her to budget her money. I personally know of several women who have no idea how much money their spouse makes. On the surface it appears that he is looking out for her by "giving" her some of *his* money, and forcing her to be a wise steward of her "allowance." But subtly, the ego is telling this man to keep his control as the man. This makes him feel superior on some level and her inferior, back to old programming and ego-based thinking. I'm aware of situations in which the woman has had to call her husband and ask permission to buy something while she's in a store. Understand of course, that some couples have the finances completely worked out between them and have decided together who handles what, but since finances are one of the leading causes of a problem relationship or divorce, it appears that most are experiencing a power struggle over finances.

Another focus of control may come with the children. One parent tells a child to do their homework, but the other parent, trying to win "favors" with the child, counteracts the first parent's instructions, allowing him to watch TV instead and saying he can do the homework later. This is very confusing for a child and describes another kind of manipulative control. Many parents use this tactic when trying to gain some kind of control with a partner who is doing too much of their own controlling. Each one is out to be top dog.

Your partner announces he is going somewhere that evening without you. It irritates you even though it's not something you would enjoy doing. You want him home with you because, after all, you are an exclusive couple now. You get quiet and distant and he feels guilty so he decides to stay home. Your actions manipulated him so that he gave up something he wanted to do. It made you feel better temporarily because you felt as if you had "won." He felt as if he had given in and maybe held some resentment toward you subconsciously. But you did some special things for him and made the evening nice, so it's all swept under the rug for now. Isn't this how relationships have to be? Compromising? Give and take? Or could it be that a complete powerful being would have no problem with a partner going off without her, or a partner feeling so secure within himself that he did what he felt was right for him regardless?

Another kind of attachment can be seen in relationships that have dissolved. One partner decided to leave and has moved on but the remaining partner can't seem to let go of the emotional pain. This person is resisting the separation and by not surrendering it for the highest and best, remains attached by codependency. This attachment keeps the individual "stuck" in a trap full of self-inflicted pain. Granted, there is a period of anger, grief and other emotions that must be worked through when a relationship disengages, but oftentimes, the attachment continues beyond a healthy recovery time-frame. In retrospect with this relationship, there was a strong thread of attachment running right through the middle of it.

Attachment keeps people together when they should have separated. Perhaps you've heard women in unhealthy relationships say "I can't live with him but I can't live without him either." So they resign themselves to this kind of life because of fear. They are afraid to be who they are and they allow their spirit to slowly die. Attachments hold people together for financial reasons, children, image, social life, security, status and a host of other reasons that stem from fear. Some like the "image" of a family setting; it's an ego boost, makes them feel like they "fit in" and portrays the "happy little family" that is socially accepting. Many times they feel trapped but are afraid to take a step forward. Is this not self-made prison?

Attachment can give us identification. I remember when I left my marriage after 32 years, I wondered where I belonged. My children were almost all grown and of course the couple things disintegrated, so I didn't fit into any of the social circles that I had before. I remember feeling that separation more than anything else. It's easy to see why many people jump right into another relationship without even taking a breath. We want to be identified with others. I'm sure that the children involved in a divorce or relationship breakup often wonder where they belong as well. This is because we base our identity on other people instead of ourselves. We really don't belong to anyone but ourselves. We came in by ourselves and will leave by ourselves. All we have is ourselves, but we've seen how attached we become to our relationships, even when they are miserable. Understand however that there are strong familial ties and that they are wonderful if each family member is complete on their own.

Some people are attached to the pain of a relationship. They are abused but keep hanging on for more. We think we don't understand how anyone can stay when they're beaten and bruised, but for these individuals, it goes right back to low self-worth. They actually believe they deserve this because they probably did something bad to provoke it and therefore it's their fault. Or perhaps someone suffers verbal abuse, which many psychologists say is even worse than physical abuse. If you are continually criticized it certainly doesn't build your self-esteem. Even if you know intellectually that your partner is only saying those things because of his own issues, hearing it over and over bores into your subconscious and becomes your reality. You begin to believe it on the subconscious level and then it creeps into conscious patterns.

Individuals who remain in these relationships may thrive on the conflict. Even if they suffer a great deal they enjoy being the victim because of the attention they receive and need. The ego tells them to hang in there because it might get better, and while they are suffering people feel sorry for them and they gain recognition for their pain. Stop and think about the times in your life you've felt this way and were lavished with sympathy and pity from friends with words like "Oh you poor thing." You probably thrived on it. Someone hurt you or used you in some rather unpleasant way. It doesn't make us feel good as we think on it now, but we've all been there at some point in our lives. Do not feel guilty or ashamed because you experienced these feelings. Just understand them and let them go, and avoid them when situations appear again.

Some people are attached to their old beliefs and programming. They hang onto them for dear life because it's all they know. It makes them feel safe and perhaps honorable if they hold the beliefs of mom and dad. I remember the story of a woman who always cut the end of a roast off and threw it away. One time her husband asked her why she did this since it seemed wasteful to throw a chunk of the roast away. Her reply was "My mom always did it so I do it." She had no idea why she was doing it, she just did it because she was following a handed-down pattern. Once she recognized her robot-like pattern she changed her action by changing her thought about what she was doing - wasting good meat!

We do this with programmed patterns from fear. Our low self-worth is a perfect example. We've been taught these ideas and have accepted them as our own. They become part of our thought consciousness and help to create the life we are experiencing. We accept them as the way it is without considering that there might be another way. So we stay in the same linear thinking of our ancestors with tunnel vision that keeps us stagnant.

Religions around the world propagate attachment. It is programmed into their followers that they must adhere to certain beliefs, rules and teachings. People adopt the beliefs and then accept them as their own. The mold is poured and we are told to fit in. I was trained in some rather rigid religious teachings. I accepted them as the way it is but often had questions to which I didn't get answers that satisfied me. But because of the fear that I would be punished if I didn't believe the way I was taught, I tried to fit the mold. Over the years, however, things weren't working and I searched for more. As I searched for more, more came. It was then that I realized I needed to establish my own belief system and not accept someone else's system. But like most attachments, it wasn't the easiest thing to do because the programming had been happening for decades. Eventually I was able to realize that I am the only one responsible for my beliefs and that it didn't matter what anyone said, I had the right to believe them. Do you know how freeing that is? Incredible!

Another part of the attachment within religion and other belief systems is that people want to be accepted within certain groups. Conformance is much easier than nonconformance. This goes back to the attachment of identity because people by nature want to belong to something, somewhere, anywhere, just so they "belong." Standing out by yourself as would happen with nonconformance creates the feeling of separation that most individuals don't wish to feel. This thread of *separational dislike* is involved in all attachments in some way.

On a deeper spiritual level, there can be attachment involved with karma. Karma is the universal law of cause and effect, what you sow you shall also reap. When Jesus taught this to his followers he was saying that whatever you put out into the universe will come back to you. In *The Path to Love,* Deepak Chopra says "The universe, under God's grace, is seen as a place where no debt goes unpaid." We have to be careful that we don't become attached to the desire for a "just reward" when someone has done something to us that we didn't like.

Karma serves only two purposes in reality: it is either a sign of love that originates from spirit or it is a lesson to be learned in love. It might be difficult for many people to come from this space of love when we see someone "getting away" with their misdeeds as they accumulate obvious "bad" karma. Of course, in reality there is no "bad" karma since it is either a lesson or an example of love. Every human being is also a divine being so that a person who "erred" is just as much a saint as you are. The universe is the controller for what comes back and when, not us. *That makes nonattachment the most valid expression of love.*

Attachment to an outcome is a common control technique we use. We envision it and decide the way things should be. The trouble lies in the detail because we want to guide God with our perception of the *how.* And we're so good at this too! We get right in the middle voicing our "opinions," and then worry and stew and anxiously await the steps to unfold. No matter how much we contrive and manipulate the course of events, it works exactly the way it was meant to work. Just think of all the energy wasted on those derivatives of fear!

Let's look at an example of getting in the way. A friend and I had been guided to work on a book together. She was contributing spiritual guidance and confirmation from this information I was receiving. It was powerful stuff and we were both excited about making the words flow to the paper, but I will confess that I was pushing to spend many hours so we could get it accomplished on what I was convinced was a divine time schedule. Then suddenly, without warning, she called and said she couldn't do it, with basically no explanation. I was baffled and heartsick. I went through some anger and hurt, then sadness, but was told by my guides not to worry because all was in divine order. I guess what I had the most trouble comprehending was the sudden overnight change, and it literally had been overnight. But I then received guidance that this was her stuff and I would be moving along alone, and that she would be back eventually. I didn't understand how it would work but I let it go, finally.

Once I totally let it go, within days the message came through that I was to put everything else on the back burner and write the book you are reading. I was told that this book had to happen first for a very specific reason, and that the book would come in fast. Then it was shared with me that after the completion of this book I would finish the one I had been working on, with or without my friend. So it all became clear and I didn't need to understand why. It only required completely letting go of the outcome that I had pictured and trusting divine order. Of course I just smiled as I realized I'd fallen into my own trap one more time, but I also felt proud that I figured it out a little quicker than the previous occasion. I am known to have a stubborn streak!

An individual can be attached to almost anything, and anything to which we are attached is bondage. In bondage we are not free to express as the person we are. In bondage our lives are operated through another person's eyes, and our thoughts are controlled by that person, creating a life that isn't ours. We can be attached to money, power, success, survival, relationships, status, recognition, self-pity, pain, conflict, memories or the control itself. All of this comes from fear as we've discussed again and again, but a controlling person will usually appear to be free of fear. This is the biggest façade of all. They tell the world they are fearless but are fooling themselves most of all.

People who control other people are merely trying to cover up their own insecurities and imperfections. Psychology teaches us about many kinds of behavior as control indicators: perfectionism, possessiveness, greed, wanting our way, anger in opposition, expectations not met, obsession, domineering and manipulation. We are so used to these behaviors that we consider them normal reactions. But these behaviors can only occur for so long before something must give. A domineering father will eventually provoke the child in some way into rebellion. A possessive wife will eventually cause some kind of reaction from her husband and may drive him away, which is probably the very thing she was trying to avoid. A person who is a perfectionist will make others who are not feel very uncomfortable in his presence. When an individual feels the need to control life for himself or another being, it is born from spiritual desperation.

The answer to breaking away from the attachments in our life is by *allowing*. Allowing is the opposite of controlling. When we allow we do not resist the experience. We accept it as it is. This applies to relationships most of all. It means we allow our partner in the relationship to be who they are without conditions. "You don't have to act the way I want for me to love you." "I accept you as you are and allow you to be yourself." These statements are accepting and allowing and control is out of the picture. If allowing and accepting were practiced in relationships today, we would see a healing through love that would amaze us all. This would be freeing and lightening of the spirit of each individual to be true to self, and fear would be put to rest. And God can't free us until we're willing to let go!

I want to conclude the chapter on attachment with another
quote from Deepak Chopra's book, *The Path to Love.*

*"Attachment is a form of dependency based on ego; love is
nonattachment based on spirit. The more nonattached you are,
the more you can truly love. Action that does not bind comes
directly from love; all other action comes indirectly
from the past."*

Review

1. Attachment means to join or connect to.
*We become attached to our relationships and all the negativity that often goes hand in hand with it. We do this because we are lacking and wish for the other person to fill the void.
We call this love.*

✧

2. Attachment gives us identity.
People thrive on identity. We want to belong to someone. As a result people hang onto relationships that died long ago.

✧

3. Some people are attached to pain.
It doesn't seem possible yet people attach to the pain of a relationship. It makes them the victim and so people give empathy and pity, which fills their immediate need of attention.

✧

4. The way to free yourself of an attachment is through allowing.
Allowing means we stop trying to control and therefore stop resisting. It means acceptance of whatever comes. It frees the spirit of each individual so they can be true to themselves.

Empowerment Activity

Are you hanging on too tight? Check all that apply to you.
The negative pattern is shown in the right-hand column.

___ I must be in a relationship.   *neediness*

___ I contiuously share my tales of woe.   *victim*

___ I feel important as I care for people.   *low self-worth*

___ I'm not competent to support myself.   *fear*

___ My partner can't make it without me.   *codependency*

___ I always try to please.   *insecurity*

___ I've always done it this way.   *old beliefs*

___ I don't like to be different.   *powerless*

___ Social acceptance is important to me.   *identity*

___ I'm not afraid of anything.   *dishonest*

___ I always strive for perfection.   *shame*

Affirmation

*I choose to let go of all attachments and
accept the freedom of being true to myself.*

Facts and figures,
they may give us answers,
but surrendering allows
for God's peace.

- Carolyn Porter

6

Why - Because

*R*emember those "why" questions of a young child that became quite exasperating at times? Everything you ask your child to do is replied with a "Why?" You've told your three year old to go get his shoes. "Why?" he asks. "We're getting ready to leave and you have to wear shoes." "Why?" "Because if you don't wear shoes you might step on something sharp and cut your foot." Child says, "Why?" And the dialogue continues until Mom, in exasperation, says "Just because. Now hurry up or we'll have to leave you." And the little child runs off to get his shoes since he knows Mom's tone and that he'd better move it.

Some years ago as I was coming to a stop light in our van, one of my children pointed to a man standing by the side of the road with a cardboard sign that asked for food money. My child commented about how sad it was that the man had to stand by the road in hopes of getting money for food. One of my younger children asked "Why?" Another one answered "Because he doesn't have a home and needs a job." Another "why" came from the back seat, to which another child said "He doesn't have any money." Again came the "why" and the dialogue continued until one of my teenagers started answering "because" to every "why." Finally one of the older kids said, "Be quiet. You ask too many questions." And there it ended with a pout expressing itself on the face of the "why" child.

Don't we do this to God? When something doesn't go the way we want we ask "Why God?" The relationship was going so well and now it's over and we want to know why. We don't understand. It was meant to last for a lifetime. It doesn't matter what the challenge is - a relationship, finances, job, friendship, children or health - we so often want to know why. We analyze and pull it apart thinking that if we had done something differently maybe it would have worked, usually putting blame on ourselves or our former partner in the process. We believe that if we could just understand the *reason* it would somehow be easier. How many times have you said those words? We've all been there, many times, wanting an answer that satisfies the "why's."

What do you think God thinks of all of our why questions? We've been told so many times that God is all-powerful and only love, so why don't we *know* that all is in perfection, that God will only allow what's best for us. When we continually want to receive answers and we've already been told to have faith, I think God smiles at our silliness until finally we might hear somewhere in the stillness "Be quiet. You ask too many questions."

It is our natural propensity to analyze and assemble the facts. We seek to examine the constituents of the situation in order to determine what went wrong. In the process we become the victim again and hurt, blame, guilt, anger, resentment, bitterness and a whole host of fear-based emotions thrive in us. We line everything up in a row seeing which fits as an explanation. As we proceed through the analysis of the situation, we are looking through a very narrow tunnel, for we are seeing through the eyes of limited perception. We've been here before and feel as if we know the way. But things seem a little different suddenly. The tunnel is dark and you can hardly see anything. You are afraid. You don't understand because you've explored this tunnel before and you were sure you made the correct turn. So you begin analyzing. You came in the entrance of the tunnel as you always do so where did you make the wrong turn? There isn't any food. It's getting colder and if you can't find your way out you could freeze to death. It's scary being alone. You wonder how you ended up in this mess. You become irritated as you try to figure it out. You blame yourself and are getting angrier by the minute, imagining all the negative possibilities as you live and breathe in fear.

You have a decision to make whether you want to or not. Either you remain in fear, anger and blame or you begin moving forward to find your way out. You can ask over and over why you are in this situation and where you went wrong in what began as a fun adventure, or you can grab onto faith and continue through the tunnel. You decide to accept the situation but not remain in it, and as you begin through the tunnel there suddenly appears a faint shimmering of light in the far distance. You begin to feel some excitement and pick up your pace a bit. It becomes brighter and brighter as you move toward it. The darkness is lifting. There you are, at the end of the tunnel and light is glistening everywhere, illuminating the path and almost blinding you. You look back at the tunnel not even recognizing it because of the brightness of the light. It doesn't look so bad now and you realize how much stronger you are for going through that experience.

Oftentimes in our journey through life we find ourselves in the same situation. We're in a tight spot financially and we ask "Why is this happening to me again?" Dr. Michael Rice, in his book appropriately entitled *Why Is This Happening To Me...Again?!*, says that we have the most amazing capacity for recreating the same negative situations because we continually trigger the same old patterns. We've discussed multiple times how our thoughts are energy that create our lives. If something is happening to us again, we are focusing energy into the same old thought process. We must take the responsibility to make changes if we want a different outcome and it all begins with our thoughts and feelings. But no matter what change we desire to make, we first must surrender our will for the situation.

So let's look at a financial dilemma since more than likely you've either been there a time or two, or perhaps you're there now. You're living above your means and you know it but don't know how to correct it. Your thought process is from the consciousness of lack and you figure it's always been this way so how can it change. You whine to God with a great big "Why is this happening to me again?" when it's because you didn't listen the last time. So once again God tells you that the universe is abundant and you are prosperous. You're stuck in the quicksand of disbelief so you're preventing the abundance from reaching you. In fact, the better you are at re-experiencing your past, the better you'll become at doing just that— re-experiencing your past! And guess where it all begins. It begins in your thoughts because you are drawing to you exactly what your mind is thinking!

You must hold yourself accountable for where you are in any situation, positive or negative. The results are simply the creation of your behaviors. People like to make others accountable because it doesn't feel good when it's back on your shoulder. And yet there can only be change when the individual accepts responsibility for what is happening. We are good at reliving the same experience but expecting a different outcome. It's been said that that's insanity!

When we don't "get" the lessons from an experience in our life, we have to repeat it until we do "get it." And as long as we think the same thoughts we'll continually recreate the exact same experience, whether we want it or not. It's the universal energy that sends out and brings back the same vibration, like a reflection of a mirror.

So how do you change your thoughts from the victim to the powerful master? The first step is to be *grateful* for where you are, who you are and what you have. In order to attract more you have to reflect abundance - the mirror effect. And you really are abundant at this moment. The old habit of focusing on the bad things is extremely hard to break. But once you focus on the abundance your life will seem abundant and always in the focus. After gratitude comes *forgiving,* starting with yourself. Forgive yourself for losing faith and experiencing a repeat performance. Forgiveness gives way to love, for you must begin by loving yourself and accepting yourself just as you are. Instead of asking God "Why is this happening to me again?," say "Thank you for this lesson. Now how can I get out of this situation?" Then the fun begins because if you're really serious about changing your experiences; I can promise you new experiences will immediately show up to prove your sincerity. *Surrender them and ask for the capabilities to remedy the situation, then get out of the way!*

Be ready to *move.* Once you've committed to change it's time to take some steps. You know you cannot be financially stable unless you change your patterns. Quit spending outside of your means. Make a plan for paying off debt. Curb your spending, downsizing if necessary, establish money for the future and most importantly, shift your thoughts to the *knowing* that you can create whatever it is you want. When thoughts creep into your consciousness that your money is short or you don't think you'll ever get ahead, immediately shift to positive energy vibrations such as "I am abundant and am

making progress for financial stability in my life." Don't expect it to happen overnight, but one little step at a time. That's how successful living is accomplished - slow and steady steps. Amazingly, as you begin taking the steps in a new direction, your power will be evident.

Another important point is that the "why's" are feeding our ego. We are in essence trying to control our lives and control is always from ego. The ego is a master of delusion and tells us it is essential to our peace of mind to know the answers. Isn't it time to let go of the "why" questions and the "because" answers. We don't need to know the why. It doesn't matter. Even if we know the reason, it doesn't change the fact that it is the way it is. The key ingredient is knowing that all is in perfection and that everything happens for a precise reason. Remember your high school sweetheart? You were so in love! But you broke up, and even though you thought it was the end of the world at that time, you looked back years later and wondered what you ever saw in that person. Or you're in a career dilemma. Maybe you lost your job and are suffering from the biggest delusional fear trip. But suddenly a new opportunity appears right out of thin air and it's better than what you could have ever imagined. So you laugh and wonder why you were afraid. Remember, fear is nothing but an illusion, and when we get out of the way so our Creator can work miracles, the miracles appear. Accepting the *not knowing* opens us to spiritual manifestations of what our souls true desires are.

When you no longer need to ask questions, you have surrendered!

"Once we truly understand that God's will is that we be happy, we no longer feel the need to ask for anything other than that God's will be done."

- Marianne Williamson, author of A Woman's Worth

Review

1. We continually ask "Why?"
*We want to understand the reason behind a situation because
we don't like what's happened.*

∽

2. Sometimes we ask "Why is this happening to me again?"
*God wants us to have faith that all is in perfection.
Things keep happening because we didn't listen.*

∽

3. When we don't get the lessons we must experience it
all over again.
We are accountable for our life. Our thoughts created it.

∽

4. To change our life experiences we must change our thoughts.
*We change by: gratitude for where and who we are, forgiving
ourselves and others, surrendering our will, and moving forward in
a new direction with divine guidance. We get out of our way.*

Empowerment Activity

Make a list of questions to which you feel the need for answers.

1. _____

2. _____

3. _____

4. _____

Realizing these "whys" are getting in your way, release them one by one to God in total surrender.

Replace the "why" with a positive statement such as:

I no longer need to know the answer to _____
because I surrendered it to God's divine order.

Affirmation

I choose to refrain from asking why as I surrender into the knowing that all is in divine order.

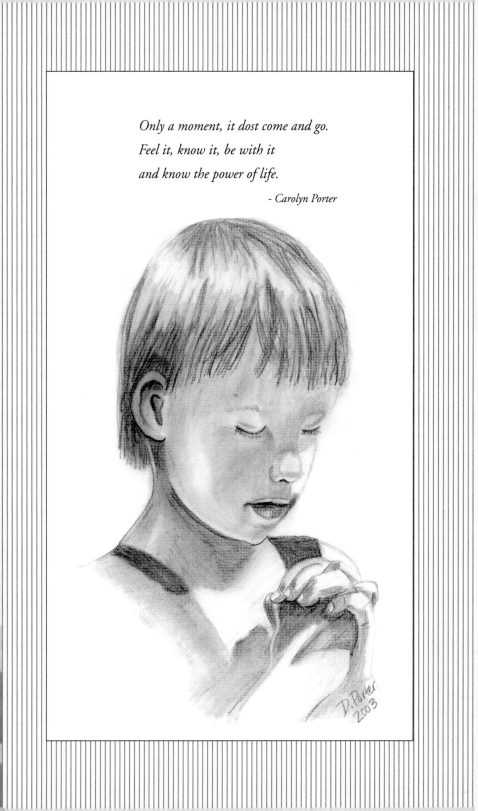

Only a moment, it dost come and go.
Feel it, know it, be with it
and know the power of life.

- Carolyn Porter

7

Just Be

I dedicate this chapter to Reverend Reginal Worrell
III, who with much wisdom and patience has continually
reminded me of my divine essence, guiding me into new
dimensions of understanding my beingness.

My Story

Reggie, as he is oftentimes referred to, was and is President
of Universal Brotherhood University. On March 5, 2000,
I was preparing to dedicate my life in service as a minister.
He had interviewed me and agreed that I was ready to
take this step. He arrived at my home where the
ceremony/service was to take place. I was preparing food
for friends and family who would be joining us for the
ceremony and I asked him repeatedly if he had everything
he needed for the ceremony. His comment was for me to

"Just be." When I continued to ask questions, he repeated that same comment several times - "Just be." He made me sit down and quit bustling about. But that wasn't my nature so when I wouldn't "Just be" he sent me upstairs until it was time for the ceremony. That was my introduction to two of the most powerful words ever uttered to me.

"To be or not to be, that is the question." Anyone raised in an English-speaking country has undoubtedly heard that quote by William Shakespeare. We rattle it off, proud that we remember something from our school days of English Literature, but probably not thinking one bit about what it could possibly mean.

What does it mean to be? Being is existing. It is in the process of becoming. It is living, and it suggests the concept of "as is." Another way to say it would be, "I am." Being means that you are honoring the present-moment awareness of you and what is at that moment. In the example of my ordination, Reggie was simply asking me to be quiet within myself and to be present in the moment. He wanted me to stop fretting about the frills of the evening and think about the true meaning of what I was about to do. Being is a state of wholeness that centers in your internal self, not the external *doing*.

Most of our lives we are *doing*, not being. We are a busy society with countless activities, responsibilities and experiences, but we rarely spend time with ourselves. We cultivate family ties, friendships, business connections and continually interact with these individuals. We are a success-oriented community who is a pressing, striving, attaining, creating, achieving, driving force that is busy *doing*. Is this not but a means to an end? Trying to fulfill that emptiness with the success of short-lived pleasures? Does acquiring more make you complete and whole? Most people do their best to avoid time with themselves. We have been so conditioned into busyness and achieving that we don't stop long enough or even have the desire to stop and reach into ourselves to know who we are. We're so busy doing, that we don't understand being.

All of my life I have loved to be busy. The more I have on my plate, the more I can get done. That's not bad in itself. It's only bad if it's not balanced with time for being. As a mother of five I often found myself multi-tasking because I was also a piano teacher, decorator, and seamstress among other things. Of course, having five kids created a busyness of its own. I got lost during those years. In recent years I found myself working with someone who was a workaholic in a sense I'd never known before. I loved it! Once again, I was too busy to take much time for being. Amazingly, this was exactly the time when my life began opening up to who I am. I realized my purpose and began to understand for the first time in my life that I wanted to serve humanity.

But it wasn't until I left this working relationship and reflected on the unending hours of work, that I realized the importance of taking time to just be. Be with myself and God. Sit quietly and do nothing. Sit in silence and listen. Be in nature. Be in the now. Be in the moment. No words. No conscious thoughts. Nothing but being. For it's only in the silence that you can understand the essence of who you are. "Be still and know that I am God" allows you the knowingness of you.

The present is all we have, but we spend most of our time either in past regrets or future dreams. It's definitely important to plan and dream for the future and then move forward with those steps, but since the present moment is all we ever have, the future can be an escape from the unsatisfactory present. We deceive ourselves into believing that when we get that perfect job, or find the perfect partner, gain more wealth, then we'll be successful, happy, and complete. Our future is shaped by the quality of our consciousness

in the present, another reason for the importance of being.

So what does *just be* actually entail? It means go within and be with yourself. It's about no one else but you - your thoughts, your feelings, your values, your spirituality, your divine connection, your beliefs. It might look like silently sitting in nature, taking a walk, meditating, sitting quietly in your special space, listening - whatever works to quiet your mind. It means aloneness, solitude, oneness, self-observation, self-awareness, self love. It means being present in the moment, not thinking about what you need to do next, but being present in the moment that is now. It means to rise above consciousness and therefore above thought. It is inner stillness, and it is where we connect with Spirit.

For most of us this is a vulnerable place to be. What might we discover about ourselves if we are still? What might we see about our lives that we need to change? What wounds might be seen that we don't want to face? The ego jumps in telling us we're too busy for this. We convince ourselves that this is so and we go on with our busy lives. Yet people are searching for more - more fulfillment, more wholeness, more spirituality, more divine oneness and more love. And where can this be found? When you go within to your soul and just be. As Thich Nhat Hanh states through his teachings in *The Miracle of Mindfulness,* "Mindfulness is the miracle by which we master and restore ourselves." Mindfulness is just being.

In the space of just being, we are becoming. Becoming is the journey on our spiritual path to fulfillment and joy and eternal happiness. Becoming is a continual, never-ending life-long process of expansion and growth of our spirit. It is the transformation from earthly viewpoints to spiritual enlightenment. It is the evolving to higher vibrations of divine understanding. It is impossible to accomplish this expansion when we are in busyness. Busyness covers up our soul. Our minds must be still in order to just be. *Inner stillness is the root of personal power.*

As a person who liked to be in control of my life and who thrived on busyness, this was difficult for me to perceive. How can one just sit quietly and not think? How can one be present in the moment with no thought so that we rise above thought? Or how can one enjoy being still with yourself? It was definitely a challenge at first, but as I continually set aside time for stillness, amazing things began to occur. Unbelievable *messages* were coming through and were actually happening in life experiences exactly as I had been told. I began to *see* things about myself and other people in those still moments. I found a peace I'd never known before and a extraordinary connection with the Divine Energy from whence my power is. My world opened up and possibilities beyond anything I could have imagined came into my reality. Enlightenment in all dimensions unfolded in the right timing. My life was transforming. And it all began with just being.

My books come in this way. I get quiet and ask for divine inspiration and the words pour in. The key is to listen. I was working on two other books when one morning as I was taking a shower, the message came to write this book. It startled me because I was working on the other two and wondered why the urgency of this book; I was told to put the others on the back burner and move forward with this one. I listened and followed my guidance without hesitation because I've learned it's the only way for me. Some days my schedule would suddenly change with cancellations or something similar. Then it would come to me to write. So I did and I'd always smile at how perfect every circumstance is when we allow ourselves to just be with it.

This is part of being, accepting all as is. When circumstances suddenly change, we must accept as is and just be with it, for it's all part of the divine plan. Even when things aren't what we want or expect, you can be with the knowing it is perfect. It may not be clear until you reflect at a later time, but it is in peace that we can

accept it without judgment or resistance.

In our busy pace of life we live fast, trying to accumulate all the worldly things we can - family, wealth, success, friends, recognition, worth, fun. Why not consider another way? Live deep. Go within and find your inner resources in order to know you. Jesus asked the question of his followers "What shall it profit a man if he gains the whole world and loses his soul?" Take time to understand the joy of living from the heart. Anything less than living from your heartspace is living a façade no matter how much money you make, how successful your career is or how many toys you have. Do you remember the old cliché, "Money can't buy you love?" It can't.

The communion with God and spiritual guidance that is available to every person alive on this planet, comes with just being. Each of you can find this same space of being. It begins with willingness. Deciding that you will find time for stillness and just be with yourself is indicating your willingness to transform areas in your life and find yourself. It's about creating space for you and accepting your responsibility of becoming which allows unlimited possibilities in your life. It's a realm unknown to most but where all masterpieces are created, especially the masterpiece called *You!*

As you experience just being, you will be able to ascertain qualities within yourself and a knowingness of your spirit that were not evident to you at previous times. The quietness will calm the mind chatter and you will reach a new plateau of enlightenment. You will begin to know your greatness and that you are already powerful with unlimited potential. Your low self-esteem will gradually fall away and be replaced with your own worthiness. You will be falling in love with yourself. And the day will come that you will enjoy being with just you. I can emphatically say that I now enjoy my own company!

"*The more tranquil a man becomes, the greater is his success, his influence, his power for good. Calmness of mind is one of the beautiful jewels of wisdom.*"

- James Allen, author of "As A Man Thinketh"

Review

1. Just Be is a state of existing, being "as is."

✌

2. Our lives are about *doing* instead of being.
*We are a busy society who bustle about with so much
busyness that we don't take time to find ourselves.*

✌

3. Being means to live in the present moment.
*We often live in past regrets or future dreams, but all we really
have is the now.*

✌

4. Stillness is a vulnerable place to be.
*Generally people don't like to feel vulnerable; it is
uncomfortable. It involves looking within and many
are afraid of what they might see.*

✌

5. When quiet, divine inspirations come through.
*This is where the spirit expands and is transformed.
In the stillness you find God.*

Empowerment Activity

Check the activities appropriate for you to allow stillness
into your life.

___ meditation ___ yoga

___ prayer ___ take a bath

___ journaling ___ lay in your hammock

___ sitting in nature ___ walking in nature

___ floating on a raft in a pool ___ listening to quieting music

___ other _____ ___ other _____

Commit to incorporating three of these into your life now.

1. _____ 2. _____ 3. _____

Affirmation

I choose to take time for stillness
for there I expand my beingness.

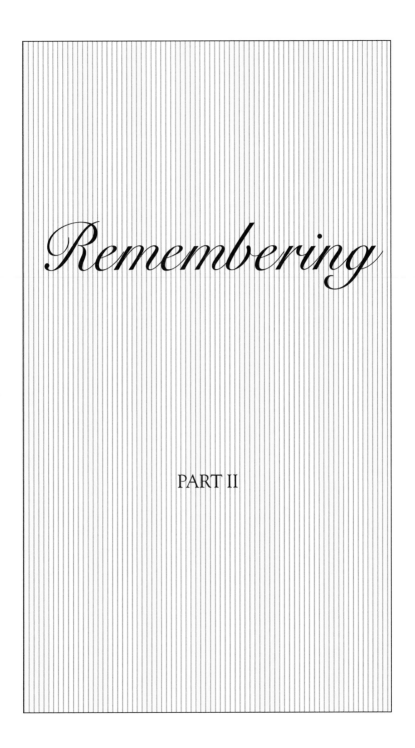

Remembering

PART II

In the stillness of timeless time

spirit speaks.

Listen reverently to the voice of your greatness.

— Carolyn Porter

8
I'm Okay

From the time we were little tykes we've been told
we're not okay unless we behaved a certain way. We learned
that we needed to put our toys away to be okay. When our
report card was less than what mom and dad wanted, we
probably felt their disapproval and absorbed the message that
we weren't good enough. We soon learned that we were either
too thin, too fat, too tall, too short, or that our hair was too
straight, too curly, or the wrong color. Shame on us if we
weren't coordinated enough to be a sports star or make the
cheerleading squad because those things were "it." And if
we had to buy a ten year old car we would never make the
"in" crowd. If we weren't popular, if we were on the outside
looking in, we weren't okay. If we didn't graduate with honors,
we weren't okay. How much salary did we make compared
to our friends? Did we measure up or not? The message came
through loud and clear that we are defective!

That mindset of being defective was carried into adulthood. Can we impress people with our exterior - our physical appearance, image, status, career or charm? Are we able to portray our façade effectively enough to fool the world into believing this is who we are? Are we able to live in delusion so well that we actually believe it's real? And how long can we sustain this? At what point does it break our spirit? At what point do we realize that we are unhappy and unfulfilled?

For most of my life I felt unworthy. I didn't think I deserved anything good because I wasn't good - I was a sinner and therefore unworthy of God's love. I used to question that belief but I had no answer. My religious upbringing taught me that I was unworthy and undeserving of anything good and I accepted it - it was all I knew. I transported that consciousness through the years and continually saw my flaws. No matter how many "good" things I did or how much I accomplished it was never enough. I tried over and over to become good enough, often burning the candle at both ends to produce more and become better. But it didn't work and I remained defective in my thoughts. Many of you experienced the same thoughts throughout your life and may be experiencing them presently.

As I grew with my spiritual awareness I began to realize that this thought process was of man. There is God, Creator, Higher Power, Universal Energy Force, who is only love. Since God is only love then it isn't possible for God to create anything that isn't love. This makes you and I pure love, radiating outwardly to all the world the essence of our being. We are not flawed. We stand in perfection as a mirror of Divine Love. But even if we understand this principle with our minds, our programming of imperfection has been so intense that our patterns of experiencing life depict a deeper belief that we are defective and therefore don't deserve the wonderful abundance of life. We are sabotaging ourselves and blocking all the good things from coming to us. And yet the whole time we are striving to become good enough, we are already perfect!

So the old belief of low self-worth appears on the scene once again. This is the root of it's foundation, the belief in our own unworthiness. We may even go a step further and call it self-loathing. In *Something More,* Sarah Ban Breathnach says

> "Self-loathing is grief that has festered; the rampant infection of self-pity. To loathe something or someone is 'to detest' with just enough disgust and intolerance to make the feeling the emotional equivalent of roiling rot. This is what self-loathing is." How many of you, if you look deep inside, loathe something about yourself?

We must go back to the basics and see our essence as love, unconditionally given, and as co-creators with God we are in perfection. As we change our concepts and accept ourselves as divine love, we then see our value as divine beings in this world. How could we be anything else? Loving ourselves is where we begin so that we can send that love out from within us to everyone in our lives. We cannot accomplish this without first being the love in us.

Now we know that we are perfection straight from God, fully loaded with wonderful gifts that are waiting to unfold. It's time to acknowledge our worthiness and believe it deep in our souls, for it  is truth. We deserve to have whatever is our highest and best for we are part of God's Universe which is abundant with treasures for all who allow them in. It's time to rejoice in who you are right now, standing in all your glory as you are. And it's time to allow the best of life to flow to you as its rightful heir. Following is a quote from *A Woman's Worth* by Marianne Williamson that shares with us how to be joyful in the knowing of our beingness.

> "Let us seek all that is true and loving and good about

womanhood. We ask for wisdom and guidance that we might reach the highest vibration of humanity of which we are capable, praying to be shown what we do not know and to be the women that God would have us to be. From there we shall know joy, and this is what we were born for.

Joy is our goal, our destiny. We cannot know who we are except in joy. Not knowing joy, we do not know ourselves. When we are without joy, we grope in the dark. When we are centered in joy, we attain our wisdom. A joyful woman, by merely being, says it all. The world is terrified of joyful women. Make a stand, be one anyway.

Joy is what happens when we allow ourselves to recognize how good things are and to see that God's plan is perfect and we're already starring in a perfect show. It demands that we have the audacity to embrace the knowledge of just how beautiful we really are and how infinitely powerful we are right now...without changing a thing - through the grace that's constantly born and reborn within us.

Our deciding to be joyful demonstrates our willingness to relinquish the petty and negative preoccupations that stand in its way. When we give these up, a more joyful life has a chance to emerge. So, let's give up and know joy!"

That's the synopsis. If we give up the self-condemnation we can become joyful with who we already are. This creates a flow of like energy emitting from us to others and returning like the pebble in the pond. When you throw a pebble in a pond the ripples slowly find the other shore, but if you wait long enough the ripples will return to you, subtly though, for they return underneath the water's surface. We may not always visibly see how our loving energy effects another's life, but we will always experience the return of whatever we send out in some form. Wouldn't you rather attract people into your life that reflect your greatness instead of your perceived unworthiness?

Begin with gratitude, gratefulness for everything about you, and I mean *everything.* It doesn't matter the size of your hips, how big your house is, whether you own a lake house, or how many dates you get; these are externals. You are a perfect creation with worth beyond measure. Often in my seminars I ask my audience to write down ten things about themselves that are wonderful - values, talents, gifts - internal qualities. You might think that ten isn't many. That's what I thought, too, but I am amazed that some people can't come up with more than five. Perhaps you would profit from taking a moment right now to write down on paper ten things about you that are wonderful. Once you write the ten, keep the paper and re-read these ten every day until you believe in your own worth.

Acceptance

Acceptance means to approve, so when we accept ourselves as we are, we are approving God's handiwork! If we loath ourselves we are saying God messed up. Does God really mess up? That's our misguided perception for sure. So if we're already okay just as we are, then we need to change our beliefs about our defectiveness.

We have the freedom and the capability to change things so they serve our highest and best. We can start this process by taking inventory of anything we don't like about ourselves. This can apply to our physical being, our thoughts, emotional responses and our spiritual connection.

First of all, make a list and ask yourself "What don't I like about myself (or my life)?" Then ask the following questions of each thing on the list.

1. Do I want to change this?

2. Can I change this?

3. How would I change this?

4. How can I accept what I can't or don't want to change?

Let's run through some examples using these questions so you understand how the format works. We'll begin with the subject of aging. Most people don't want to age. Our society places such emphasis on youthfulness with the perception that once you reach a certain age you are over the hill and pretty much on a downward spiral for the rest of your life. Yet some societies revere their elderly so highly that we find these people living long lives that are healthy and active all way through. It's all in perception and belief.

We establish that we don't like the signs of aging we are seeing externally. So we can ask if we want to change any of these telltale signs. We decide we'd like to get rid of the wrinkles on our face and also the love handles that wrap around our waist. Maybe we'd also like to look deeper into healthy food intake for insuring good nutrition necessary to fight aging.

The next question is, "Can I change this?" Sure you can. The next question is how to change it. The love handles can be remedied with lifestyle changes of diet and exercise, and the healthy food intake may require some reading or classes for understanding and information. Proper diet will reduce some of the wrinkles or you could just find a reputable surgeon and get rid of them all. But then you must accept the fact that you aren't twenty any more and never will be again in this life. You can fix your face temporarily, reduce your fat accumulation, and change to a healthier diet, but you are still going to get older in chronological years. You can't stop this process so you must accept it, but you can learn much on how to create quality in your life as you age. How you respond to these facts makes all the difference.

Are you asking "If we believe in our perfection then why would we want to change anything about ourselves?" "Isn't that a contradiction if we're already perfect?" Remember through whose eyes you are seeing yourself. Each person has their own perception. And we haven't always made the best choices about ourselves and our life. We have free will to make changes. The only problem that we might encounter is if we feel the need to make these changes in order to feel better about who we are. It's a fine line. At which point do we *need* to make the changes to feel better about ourselves versus changing things that can be for our highest and best. Always ask yourself this question: "If I change this will it be for my highest and best and help me on my path of purpose?" There is certainly value in looking and being our best, but no matter how good we fix up the external form, it is our heart that makes us who we are, and that's what people want to see. It's okay to make changes as long as they aren't a measure of your worth.

I've had to deal with this process. I used to ask God why he didn't transform my life when I was 30 so I'd have more years to serve others and share my message. I didn't hear the answer for a while because I was so busy complaining and resisting the process. Then when I heard the answer I just smiled at the perfection of the timing. God wants me to reach women from mid-life on since that is where I am. If I was 30 it wouldn't work because the experiences and lessons I am sharing could only come with maturing years. Apparently this is part of my mission in life. Once I accepted this as okay I looked at myself differently. There are things I want to change and I have a plan to do them, but no longer do I feel less of a person because of a line or my 30+ years. These are only externals and they are not who I really am within.

In the illustration above, this person wants to change signs of aging with rejuvenation of the face. Why not? Why not take advantage of the wonderful abilities that many surgeons have made available through years of study and new technology? Could that be for our highest and best if it improves our appearance? And the dietary changes to reduce fat and provide healthier food for our body is certainly something for our highest and best from a health standpoint as well as from our self-image. I say go for whatever you desire to improve your life. But don't forget that the most important aspect of acceptance followed by change must be about the continuous internal acceptance of where and who we are, and realizing that coming back to love is an on-going process throughout our lives. We came from love and so are in perfection, but when we came into human form in this lifetime we have forgotten that love and we are in the continual evolution of remembering that love and returning to it. There is the key to the changes we desire to make in our lives: if we are always seeking the love from whence we came, we will know what choices and changes are good for us that promote our highest devotion to that love. And we will know we are okay.

Let's look at finances. Perhaps you've found yourself in an undesirable financial situation. You have tried to get ahead but somehow it doesn't happen. Why is this happening again? You don't like it! So let's begin at the beginning. Most assuredly you were brought up with the established thoughts of lack - never enough, can't buy it, must be frugal, money is the root of all evil, things aren't important, money doesn't grow on trees. You were programmed with these thoughts so you are simply carrying them into your life experience.

The first step is accepting where you are and being grateful for all that you have. You are abundant even if you have financial challenges, you just may not see it in your present circumstances. Beginning with gratitude places emphasis on the positive instead of on your perceived negative circumstances. It will immediately begin shifting your thoughts from lack and want to abundance and plenty. Then you have to surrender the circumstances and get out of the way, in order for the changes to happen.

One time when I was experiencing a new path that required some patience in making things happen financially, I joined in a conversation about financial difficulties. I casually mentioned that things were tight for me as well. A male friend turned to me (he knew a little of my situation and knew I was moving forward rather quickly in my new endeavors) and asked me what was the worst thing that could happen to me. I replied "To lose my house." He then asked "Would you survive?" I laughed and said "Of course." I got it! I got it because I realized that God had never let me down in my entire life even when I wasn't discerning with my choices, and I would survive no matter what it looked like. I am living my purpose and am a willing servant who needed to remember my abundance - the abundance of love instead of coming from fear.

So let's use the questions again and see how this fits. First of all, do you really - and I mean really - want to change this? You might say you do but at the inner core of your beliefs do you really want to? This would mean making some big changes in your lifestyle, maybe even very uncomfortable changes. Once you decide that you'll do anything to change your behavioral pattern of lack, you're ready to start the process.

Can you change this? Of course you can; it's your choice. Now for the how. It may look like a plan that includes cutting down the spending, beginning a savings plan for both emergencies and the future, paying off debt, and perhaps even downsizing your living quarters. Remember, you said you were ready to make changes. You may need to engage some professionals who can help you understand and re-program your thoughts to new ones of abundance. Change sometimes is difficult, but necessary for growth. Once your plan is set you must of course follow through, which is the toughest part.

Are you a workaholic? Do you work long hours with little time for relaxation or playtime? Are you driven to succeed and produce beyond most people's capacity? People who operate at this level are feeding their ego and trying hard to feel better about themselves. They justify the long hours by saying there's no one else to do it or no one who can do it better. That's ego. If they work long hours they're too occupied to take time to think about their insecurities or fears or shame or anger or low self-esteem. I'm not saying that it isn't good to work hard, for we know that to build something worthwhile it takes much work, but if this becomes a way of life it is simply a means of covering up the emptiness within ourselves. As we read in the previous chapter, we are busy doing instead of being.

No matter what we look like, what our lives are like, what problems we are facing, it all begins by accepting everything as is. This doesn't mean that we must resign ourselves to not allowing anything to change. *Accepting does not mean giving up or giving in, it simply means that we recognize and accept the validity of what we see.* Once we have accepted and acknowledged what is in front of us, only then can we proceed to make changes. Recognizing the validity of what we see relinquishes the self-condemnation targeted at ourselves and takes us away from fear and back on the track to love.

When we accept whatever we see without self-loathing, and we allow for the transformation to take place, then we are in the process of healing. The healing process is one of loving ourselves without judgment and the usual self-incrimination so that we can consciously change our perception from our old beliefs about ourselves. This is very important for our growth into the conscious acceptance of our greatness and power that is our birthright. Charles Whitfield, M.D., author of *Healing the Child Within*, states this truth when he writes, "My sense is that Unconditional Love is the most powerful healing and creative energy in the universe. And that Love energy exists naturally inside of each of us." Love yourself as you are because you're okay!

In the eyes of spirit you are always enough!

"God grant me the serenity to accept the things I cannot change, courage to change the things I can, and the wisdom to know the difference."

- The Serenity Prayer

Review

1. As children we are usually taught we're not okay.
*We grow up feeling flawed and defective so we take
that low self-worth into adulthood.*

✑

2. God created us in perfection.
*God is Divine Love and we are an expression of God,
making us love and worthy.*

✑

3. Begin with gratitude.
*Being grateful for who we are and what we have shifts our
thoughts to loving, positive thoughts.*

✑

4. Acceptance is necessary.
*We first must accept all things as they are - appearance,
health, finances, etc.*

✑

5. Accepting doesn't mean resigning ourselves that it must
be a certain way.
*We always have free will and can make changes.
They should always be for our highest and best.*

✑

6. Recognizing the validity of what we see is vital to our growth.
Healing comes from unconditional love.

Empowerment Activity

You are a magnificent design of God. Write ten things you
love about yourself in each column.

	Physical	Emotional/Mental	Spiritual
1.			
2.			
3.			
4.			
5.			
6.			
7.			
8.			
9.			
10.			

Did you write ten? If not, go back and complete as you
remember your magnificence:
You are one with God.

Affirmation

*I choose to accept myself as perfection,
being one with God.*

A flower blooms in all its glory,

slowly it slips away.

The space between we watch and wait

'til another bloom emerges

reaching for eternal light

breathtaking, its glory opens.

- Carolyn Porter

9
The Void

This chapter is the direct result of inspirational guidance I received from a message by Matthew ParClair, Ph.D., associate minister of Unity North Church in Marietta, Georgia. My protocol has always been to jot down notes whenever someone is speaking because there is always enlightenment I will gain from what others share. I have been repeatedly blessed by his words and wish to acknowledge his loving, humble spirit and for the perfect timing of his message that day. I do believe God had something to do with it!

The senior minister of the church I attend once shared this example of letting go. She described how a trapeze artist swings from one bar to the next. He can see the new bar swinging toward him but must let go of the present bar he is grasping in order to grab the new bar that is swinging. The space between letting go of the present bar and grabbing the new bar is the void.

The void is where we grow as we transition through life experiences. We let go of something or someone and there is a "dealing with it" time. This is the time for allowing the feelings to be expressed, whether they be grief, sadness, anger, hurt, resentment, or another expression of pain. It is necessary to feel the pain or we are limiting our growth. Without having the void time the feelings get stuffed away. They may be buried but they never die and will eventually surface in some form, often as an illness.

We've been talking about the old beliefs, attitudes, programming and patterns that we must surrender and then replace with a new consciousness of our eternal greatness. This transformation of the old to the new takes place in the void. This space between forces us to take a look at the life experience we've released so that we can grow beyond it into something greater. It is a time of waiting and trusting Divine Power. It is a time to sift through the rubble and see what we can find. What valuable lessons have we learned? What wonderful memories do we have? Have we gained discernment by going through this ending?

As we sift through all the lessons and pick out what we see is worth saving, we are called to go deeper into the experience so our spirit can heal. It is where we take a good look at what's inside of us. Was not that the purpose for the relationship or the experience? It may feel like the dark night of the soul for a while, but eventually we'll come out on the other side in light and understand the value of this transition. It is in the stillness of timeless time that we can feel our feelings. Without feeling them we are denying the process of healing, so we'll more than likely repeat the entire scenario again.

When an individual leaves a relationship and goes directly into another one, they are denying the healing and growing time. The denial of the feelings causes them to be stuffed, only to be replayed in the future. There is little if any growth and the spirit hits a plateau. The feelings that this individual displays of anger, grief, resentment, sadness, depression, are all derivatives of fear. Fear is an illusion that keeps this person stuck as the feelings are buried deep into the cells' memory. There was no time for stillness in which the spirit could determine what needed to be let go and what is important to retain in the memory. Nothing has been dealt with and the person will assuredly proceed through a repeat of the same story they just ended.

We've talked about resisting situations in which we can then shift into the experience of allowing. We discussed the importance of letting go of the bondage of attachments and that we don't need every "why" question answered. All of these are in the ending phase of our life experience. They are part of the letting go process that can lift us up to higher planes of awareness. But as we enter the void stage, we must remember that as we let go of the ending, we must search for new enlightenment from love to fill up the space of void. Left vacant, negative patterns will jump right back into place to replace the old negatives you just released.

The void is a wonderful place to be, for it's here that we can grow more expansively than any other time. We have become vulnerable and when vulnerable we are ready to listen and learn. It may feel like our lives are topsy-turvy as many shifts will be taking place, especially in our base of operation. Here we re-group and get ready for the new beginning that is just over the horizon. How much sweeter will the new beginning be after the shifting, flip-flopping period of the void. And just think how much stronger you'll be as it comes to you. You can never appreciate the beauty of the rainbow until the storm has come and gone, for it is the storm that produces the beautiful rainbow. God is in the silence of the empty spaces and is ready to fill that emptiness with miracles.

In the void we learn patience, which is often a challenge to our virtues. The following quote came via an email and I have no

idea who the author is, but the words are so powerful I have it above my computer desk so I'm reminded of it daily. Patience is something I too am learning.

> "Waiting is an art; waiting achieves things. Waiting can be very powerful. Time is a valuable thing. If you can wait two years, you can sometimes achieve something that you couldn't achieve today, however hard you worked, however much money you threw up in the air, however many times you banged your head against the wall…Things happen when the time is right!"

Isn't this a wonderful written expression of what can happen during the void of our transitions? We often want what we want when we want it and we don't want to wait or go through anything unpleasant. We are a fix-it-fast society that carries through that pattern in many aspects of our life. Yet our power lies in transforming our fears into loving manifestations. Many times it requires the patience of Job and always the surrendering of our will to God. In my own life, whenever I let go of a situation and quit getting in my own way, it always worked exactly how and when it should. I always smile and think how smoothly it all worked and often better than I had imagined it could.

During our residence in the void is our space for awareness of what needs to be released. If you've just completed a relationship of some kind, there are beliefs and perceptions that you must release. One belief to release is the belief of judgment that says you did this hurtful thing to me and you should suffer. It's so easy to feel justified with blame or be the victim and forget all about divine love; our egos are masters at disguising. This is part of our healing where we flip our perceptions from the shackles of fear to the freedom of love, allowing complete forgiveness. It is only in the stillness of the void that we can come to terms with this enlightenment of our spirit. It requires deep, soulful searching and waiting to achieve.

To help you through your process of healing, try using these suggestions to transform the circumstance from all forms of fear - blame, judgment, revenge, hurt, anger, resentment, victim, to all forms of love - forgiveness, compassion, appreciation, surrender, gratitude.

1. Feel the pain of the experience. Know that it's all okay and the situation is in perfection.

2. Pick apart the experience and ask yourself why you're feeling the pain.

3. Ask yourself where you've felt this pain before and why you are allowing it once again.

4. What do I need to do to break this repetitive negative pattern?

5. Look for the gifts in this experience.

6. Put your feet in the other person's shoes for just a moment and see their point of view.

As you work through the release of the old energy and get ready to embrace the new energy, you will begin to feel the peace of God envelope you. That place of churning and thrashing about has given way to renewed energy that resonates God's love, a quiet, restful, waiting oasis. You are gaining strength and power as you gaze into the possibilities of what lies ahead. Now you are ready to be free to experience aliveness once again. Having been through the dark side of the night, the new possibilities are so much sweeter. The possibilities are endless and all you must do is look up and see them.

Become a possibilitarian. No matter how dark things seem to be or actually are, raise your sights and see possibilities - always see them, for they're always there."

- Dr. Norman Vincent Peale, author of
The Power of Positive Thinking

Review

1. The void is the space between the ending and the
new beginning.
*This is not a place we want to be, but is necessary for the
transition process.*

 ✒

2. Being in the void causes us to go deeper within.
It is here in the stillness between that we grow the most.

 ✒

3. The void is where we release the negativity of the
ending we just experienced.
*If these fears are not released in this period of void, they will be
stuffed away, very much alive, and will resurface later on.*

 ✒

4. In the waiting of the void we gain strength.
Waiting is an art and is very powerful.

 ✒

5. Use the six suggestions to help heal your process in the void.

Empowerment Activity

Think of a relationship ending you have experienced. Write
the lessons you learned and the ways in which you grew
- the gifts.

Lessons   Gifts

1. _____   _____

2. _____   _____

3. _____   _____

4. _____   _____

5. _____   _____

6. _____   _____

7. _____   _____

8. _____   _____

9. _____   _____

10. _____   _____

Affirmation

*I choose to see the void time as an incredible
gift for my growth into higher awareness.*

Dawn breaks, the sky unfolds its beauty
breathing deeply the newness of day.
Time stretches out before us
giving thought to who we are,
reaching for happiness with extended arms,
filling our lives with whatnots and things
for a time.

Happiness not eludes, for harboring within
with greatness and power unbounded,
lie gifts so unique inborn from the start,
to illumine the world with their light.

- Carolyn Porter

10

Stepping Into
Your Passion

Have you ever questioned the validity of your existence? Why exactly are you in this particular lifetime experience? Maybe you've even asked who you really are, or isn't there more to life than this? What would I really like to be doing with my life? When you ask these questions it's because you are ready to embark on a spiritual journey to find your true self. The problem, however, is that people may want answers to these questions, but sadly may never go past the thought. This chapter invites you to explore the possibility of finding passion in your life and learn the simple truth that to serve God is the true meaning of life. Our soul's purpose is much greater than we can grasp.

Each of us has a unique gift that is ours and ours alone; no one has this gift exactly the same as you do. At the moment of conception it is there, waiting to be brought out for the world to see. Most of us get so caught up in the creation of our external lives that our gift is forgotten and left buried in the shadows.

Alan Cohen shares so eloquently in his book *I Had It All the Time* how most people are experiencing life. He writes

> "Most people are dying rather than living in their work. They do not realize that *livelihood* begins with *live*. They wake up in the morning, groan at the prospect of another exhausting day, force themselves out of bed, and drag their reluctant minds and bodies to jobs that are boring at least, and abhorrent at worst. They do not realize how profoundly they are dishonoring themselves and their talents by tolerating careers in which their life force is diminished to the tiniest trickle of creativity and self-expression."

You know those "gut feelings" you sometimes feel? Those little nudgings that propel you toward something that you ignore? Maybe you're reading a book and you think, "I could write a book. In fact, I think I could expand on this even better than this guy did." You mull it over in your mind a while and even get some excitement about it, but then other thoughts creep in. "I'm so busy I really don't have time," or "I know nothing about writing a book," or " I doubt if anyone would want to read it anyway." So you toss that inner nudging away and perhaps will leave the planet with the book still inside you. You ignored your spiritual guidance. Was that to be your gift that the world is waiting for you to share, the passion that is missing in your life?

Passion is enthusiasm or strong feelings about something. It ignites an internal fire within us. Most people think of passion as sexual desire, and although that certainly fits with the definition of passion, it is short-term gratification. The passion to which I am referring is the passion about life as a whole. What is your life about? What are you doing for others? Are you enjoying what you do so much that it is fun and you can't wait to get started on it every day? Is every day oozing with enthusiasm and joy from deep within you? Is this feeling of passion on-going, never-ending? Is what you're doing for the highest and best of you, others and the planet?

When you are living on purpose you are passionate about life. Your excitement ignites the realm of your existence. Each day seems like a new adventure. It's your inner reason for being here in this life experience. It is your self expressing the gift that resides deep within that came with you. People see it in you. And when you're on purpose you are moving because of the passion you feel. Oprah says,

> "When you're living on purpose no one has to say 'Go Girl' because you've already gone."

And that's how it is. You are out there making things happen.

But so many people deny the existence of a purpose as they focus on everyday living. There are friends and family, social activities, career, earning a living, and all the other facets of life that make it reality in the physical realm. One might ask, "Who has time to worry about something deeper?" They feel already stressed and can't imagine taking on anything else. But what they don't realize is that the stress and busyness of their reality is a cover-up for the realness hidden inside. People often don't want to go there for fear of what they might see.

Then others want to know their purpose but can't figure out how to find it. They are searching but after a while they give up the search because they don't believe they can find it. They remain restless, knowing there is something greater within them, but tired of the effort needed to discover it.

All of our lives we've been told that giving to others is the most important way to show love. We give and give and give some more, but then one day we find ourselves on empty and have nothing else to give. The well ran dry. That happened to me in 1994 when I got sick. My body said, "Enough is enough, there is no more energy for you to share." I didn't know it then but it was going to take me the next five years to get well. I learned that I hadn't been taking care of myself but had given all I had to others - my family, friends, church activities, piano students, organizational activities and so on. I was out of reserve. I always thought it was more blessed to give than to receive and had given continuously from that thought consciousness. Then an interesting concept was shared with me that made so much sense. But first let me share this illustration for clarification.

Envision a giant oak tree, branches extending to the sky with masses of rich dark green leaves. The tree offers wonderful shade from the hot summer sun and gives refuge to our feathered friends. Insects reside with this tree and squirrels gather its acorns for their winter store. It stands there in all its glory, a magnificent expression of creation. But think a minute about this tree. It is providing all these services for us but how did it all begin? The tree began as a tiny acorn planted in the ground. It had to take sustenance from the earth to grow and soaked up the raindrops as well. It sprouted and began to grow toward the heavens, grabbing the sun's rays while it continued to gather nutrients from the soil and rain from the sky. After it took from the abundance of the earth - rain, soil nutrients, sun - it was able to provide mankind with gifts we could enjoy. After it was mature and able to give, it continued to take whatever it needed so that it could continually give.

This is something we have had backwards most of our life. We think we have to give first, but how can we give what we don't have? The secret is that we must fill ourselves up first so that we can overflow to others, and in this way we'll never run out. In *The Gift of Taking* Dr. Jill Kahn says this very thing "Honor yourself first; all else will follow." This is what the tree does. It fills itself up, taking from the abundance of the earth, *then* it spills over with gifts for us. If it didn't do it this way the tree would wilt and die and we would miss the wonderful gifts it has to share.

The same is true with humans. We must fill ourselves up first, listening to our spirit for guidance and always coming from a space of love. We cannot give something we do not have, and if we aren't full of love we'll never have any to share with others. Living our purpose fills us up and allows great abundance in our life.

There is nothing more important than knowing what your purpose in life is, *nothing*. In fact, when you love what you do and are on purpose it actually becomes your life. Understand that your purpose can change from time to time, that it's normal and good as you expand into higher planes of spiritual awareness, which is part of your process. What better way to fill yourself up than living your passion? You are excavating your authentic self, your spirit, who you really are, and you and your life are interchangeable.

Perhaps I've convinced you of the importance of knowing your purpose, but how do you discover what your purpose is? There are many ways to approach this and I will give you suggestions for what has worked in my life and the lives of many of my clients and friends.

The first step is to make the *decision* that you desire to find your purpose. Ask God or Higher Power to show you your purpose. By this you are saying that you are open and willing. *Make sure you really mean it.* Of course God knows your heart because you and God are one.

Then there's *commitment.* When you state you are willing it is saying that you are committing to the process and will follow through to complete the task. Many, many people begin the journey but when the going gets tough they bow out. People like to be comfortable and secure. Moving into unknown territory brings out much fear, and although it's only an illusion, it stops them abruptly in their tracks. We've already learned that fear is the biggest barrier in our lives and that holds especially true for reaching out of our comfort zone into uncharted territory.

Surrender the fear and do it anyway. You'll never make it if you don't ever begin. Letting go of the fear and self-sabotage we inflict upon ourselves will open up channels of miracles that will flow right to you. But we must give up the fear.

Here's where the beautiful word *faith* appears. Faith is necessary to step into the unknown and begin this new path. Faith is trusting God for the working of all details, no matter what. When you begin your purpose you will find some challenges along the way. There is always some risk. However, these challenges are another showering of God's gifts because they show us inner strength we didn't know we had. If there was never an obstacle how would you know the ability of your creativity to solve the problem? Through these experiences we learn to tap into resources hidden from our view.

Think of yourself as a miner, excavating the inner recesses of your soul for the diamonds. What is hidden in the shadows of your inner self? Some people find meditating very helpful in bringing in their purpose. But many people I personally know have spent years waiting for something to come through, when sometimes just using the right tools will allow it to happen sooner. It's not that we must try so hard, but that we chip away the blocks that are hiding it from our view.

When I discovered my purpose, I used a written exercise that helped me see a thread weaving through my strengths and what I loved doing. It gave me some genuine clues that opened up ideas for the direction in which I needed to move. I recreated the exercise in a way that seems more effective in helping individuals dig deeper for their spirit's answers. I have repeatedly used this simple exercise with my coaching clients in order to unlock the truth within their soul. Here is what you do.

Find a quiet place where you will *not be interrupted.* Gather two sheets of paper and a pen or pencil and set them beside you. Now relax and take several deep breaths, concentrating on the breath. Feel your body relax, sinking deeply into the chair. When ready take up your paper and begin by answering these four questions; *each question must have six answers,*

1. What do I really enjoy doing?
2. What do I do well?
3. What is important to make me feel satisfied with my life?
4. Looking inside of me, what do I believe I should contribute to this world?

Let your spirit flow through instead of using your mind. Write down whatever comes in no matter how silly it seems. After completing these four questions with a total of 24 answers, prioritize the top three answers of the six under each question by imagining which would be the most important if you only had a few years left to live. Put these answers on the second sheet of paper. As you read your answers you should see the thread weaving them together that gives a good indication of the area where your purpose is.

Some people have trouble seeing anything that makes sense to them. At that point I suggest coaching sessions by someone trained in understanding how to use this exercise. When I facilitate a complete coaching session that incorporates this exercise, I can easily see the thread, and there is no thrill greater for me than watching someone come to life as they finally see the direction in which they should move.

But many people stop right there. The ego jumps to attention and undertakes to throw rocks in your path, striving to keep the control, for beginning a new path of purpose signifies defeat for the ego. The ego's subtle efforts may include thoughts such as "You can't do that, you don't have enough time" or "You are so good at what you presently do, why would you want to change anything?

You would be letting the business down" or "Your family needs you" or "It will stress you more to add something like this," and on and on we could go. Everything the ego says is most likely true at some level, which is how it sabotages so successfully in preventing you from moving forward.

Now you need focus. This is a gift you're to give to the world so you must focus on what it is you want to do and never take your eyes off of it. If it's really what you love and you're in alignment with God's will for your life, you should be able to focus. It's your *responsibility* to do this. You came into the world with this gift to share and you won't be genuinely happy until you share it. Happiness is directly related with creativity, and living life through your purpose involves creativity - you are creating it from your spirit.

Another suggestion that has brought clarity in purpose to individuals starts by looking back over your main life experiences. Dissect the lessons, squeezing out every drop you can while you find the gifts. Look at the pattern of these experiences. Perhaps they were part of your personalized gift that you brought to share. How can you use these for good for others?

In my own life, as I looked back over many years of unhappiness, lack of self-worth, feelings of smallness, physical and emotional illness, financial struggle, unhealthy and abusive relationships with continual self-disapproval, I finally got it. I saw how every situation in my life was propelling me to where I am now, writing this book. I couldn't be writing this book unless I had lived through those life experiences and conquered them. I wouldn't be able to share insights of a victor unless I ran the difficult race. I can see how every situation in my life was part of my purpose so I could grow past that circumstance into new awareness. And that's exactly what I did. Did it hurt? Yes! Did I shed many tears? Yes! Were there times when I wanted to give up? Yes! Did I feel alone at times? Yes! But the key is that I kept going no matter what. I believe that inside on some level, even before my spiritual awakening, I knew I would make it even though I didn't understand what was happening to me.

Understanding my lessons is why I'm sharing with you in this book. Everything I'm saying was part of my learning experience because we teach what we need to learn ourselves. Each of us has our own story and our own lessons. Perhaps your story needs to be shared so others can benefit from your experiences and life lessons. What has transformed in your life from which others can benefit? Perhaps the combination of the thread that weaves through the answers in the purpose exercise and the revelations obtained by realizing your past experiences and the lessons will give you a clear picture of your passion.

Living on purpose will transform your life. It always involves change and change isn't usually easy. Sometimes you may feel alone as you enter new territory; it may mean leaving friends behind as you expand into new awareness. Somehow the common bond that kept you "dancing" as friends seems to dissipate. Bless them and be thankful for the experience of knowing and learning from them. Realize that now there will be new friends that share the same awareness that has opened to you.

As you face the wonderment of purposeful living, understand that challenges will be there, almost immediately. It's just your ego and you'll be able to walk right through its attempts of sabotage. Once you "feel" the enthusiasm that generates from within you as you touch lives, nothing will stop you. Remember that the only possibility for eternal happiness and fulfillment in this lifetime is through living on purpose. Nothing else will fill the void within you - no person or thing on this planet. So the importance of seeking your passion in life is without doubt your most urgent call to awakening. Until you know the purpose of your life and begin living it, you will experience restlessness that cannot be quieted. As you live from your passion the doors of opportunity will open, for that's how the universe is set up. We are creators and the universe brings us what we are projecting out. If we are projecting that we want to live our passion, it is guaranteed that the universe will bring all the good we desire to us. How could you ever settle for anything less than living joyously with passion?

No matter what you discover is your purpose, it is only accomplished with little, consecutive steps, one at a time. Anyone who is successful will tell you they accomplished their goals over time for no empire can be built in a day. At times you may feel like giving up. Don't! The final reward is worth more than words can ever say. You can accomplish magnificent things in your life if you believe it and move with it.

Follow your spirit! Your spirit always leads you to the higher plane of internal success where love abides, and from that place you express love. No matter how much fame or material wealth we accumulate, we will experience spiritual impoverishment unless we follow our spirit's guidance and enrich the lives of those we touch. *Your work is never about your place in the world, but rather your place in people's hearts.*

"Continuous effort - not strength or intelligence - is the key to unlocking our potential."

- Sir Winston Churchill, Former British Prime Minister

Review

1. People often wonder why they are on this planet.
Each of us has an inborn gift that we are meant to share with the world.

c**↗**↝

2. We must fill ourselves up first.
We are taught to give and give and then we wonder why we are on empty.

c**↗**↝

3. We first must decide we want to know our purpose and really mean it.
After deciding, we must commit to follow through, surrender the fear and step out in faith.

c**↗**↝

4. The simple exercise included in this chapter can help you find your purpose.

c**↗**↝

5. Ego jumps in and tries to stop your new direction.
The ego wants to keep control and will put challenges in your path. Keep on going!

Empowerment Activity

Check all that apply to you.

___ My vocation creates a passion for life.

___ I am creative in my work.

___ I look forward to each work day with excitement.

___ My work allows me to feel powerful.

___ I enjoy my work so I have a positive mood.

___ My vocation involves loving service to others.

___ I experience inner peace through my work.

___ I am not bored in my work.

___ I draw from a higher power in all that I do.

Every statement should be checked. If three or more are left unchecked, I suggest you look deeply to discover where your passion in life is and ask for God's help in aligning you with that purpose.

Affirmation

I choose willingness to find and live my passion from love.

In the face of a flower
we see God's light;
as we move forward on our path
we <u>are</u> God's light.

- Carolyn Porter

11
The Daffodil Principal

The mother of a married daughter had been repeatedly called by the daughter to make the two-hour drive to her area so she could witness the beautiful sight of a field of daffodils. The mother had put it off due to her work schedule until the daughter insisted she go then or the season would be over. She finally agreed to go a few days later.

The morning dawned cold and rainy, but she had promised so she went. The route was up a mountain highway and after a short distance she found the road was completely covered with a wet, gray blanket of fog. She slowed to a crawl and continued up the narrow, winding road with her heart pounding.

When she reached her daughter's house and greeted her grandchildren, she expressed her fright during the trip there. When the daughter said they were still going to see the daffodils she refused. She claimed that the roads were too difficult to see in the fog.

But the daughter was used to this area, driving in the fog almost daily. She persuaded her mother to take her a short distance to the mechanic shop to pick up her car. Of course she knew she would continue from the mechanic's place to show her mother the daffodils.

The daughter decided to see the daffodils before going to the mechanic, ignoring the comments of her alarmed mother as she found out her daughter's intention. The mother muttered all the way about the danger of driving that day, but suddenly they had arrived.

"We parked in a small parking lot adjoining a little stone church. From our vantage point at the top of the mountain we could see beyond us, in the mist, the crests of the San Bernardino range like the dark, humped backs of a herd of elephants. Far below us the fog-shrouded valleys, hills and flatlands stretched away to the dessert.

On the far side of the church I saw a pine-needle-covered path with towering evergreens and manzanita bushes, and an inconspicuous lettered sign 'Daffodil Garden.'

We each took a child's hand and I followed my daughter down the path as it wound through the trees. The mountain sloped away from the side of the path in irregular dips, folds and valleys like a deeply creased skirt.

Live oaks, mountain laurel, shrubs and bushes clustered in the folds, and in the gray, drizzling air the green foliage looked dark and monochromatic. I shivered. Then we turned a corner of the path and I looked up and gasped. Before me lay the most glorious sight, unexpectedly and completely splendid. It looked as though someone had taken a great vat of gold and poured it down over the mountain peak and slope where it had run into every crevice and over every rise. Even in the mist-filled air, the mountainside was radiant, clothed in massive drifts and waterfalls of daffodils. The flowers were planted in majestic, swirling patterns, great ribbons and swaths of deep orange, white, lemon yellow, salmon pink, saffron and butter yellow.

Each different-colored variety (I learned later there were more than 35 varieties of daffodils in this vast display) was planted as a group so that it swirled and flowed like its own river with its own unique hue.

In the center of this incredible and dazzling display of gold, a great cascade of purple grape hyacinth flowed down like a waterfall of blossoms framed in its own rock-lined basin, weaving through the brilliant daffodils. A charming path wound throughout the garden. There were several resting stations, paved with stone and furnished with Victorian wooden benches and great tubs of coral and carmine tulips. As though this were not magnificent enough, Mother Nature had to add her own grace note - above the daffodils a bevy of western bluebirds flitted and darted, flashing their brilliance. These charming little birds are the color of sapphires with breasts of magenta red. As they danced in the air, their colors were truly like jewels above the glowing daffodils. The effect was spectacular.

It did not matter that the sun was not shining. The brilliance of the daffodils was like the glow of the brightest sunlit day. Words, wonderful as they are, simply cannot describe the incredible beauty of that flower-bedecked mountain top. Five acres of flowers! 'But who has done this?' I asked my daughter. I was overflowing with gratitude that she had brought me - even against my will.

My daughter replied, 'It's just one woman. She lives on the property. That's her home' she said as she pointed to a well-kept A-frame house that looked small and modest in the midst of all that glory.

We walked up to the house, my mind buzzing with questions. On the patio we saw a poster. 'Answer to the Questions I Know

You Are Asking' was the headline. The first answer was a simple one. '50,000 bulbs,' it read. The second answer was, 'One at a time, by one woman, two hands, two feet, and a very little brain.' The third answer was, 'Began in 1958.'

There it was - The Daffodil Principle.

For me that moment was a life-changing experience. I thought of this woman whom I had never met, who, more than 35 years before had begun, one bulb at a time, to bring her vision of beauty and joy to an obscure mountain top - one bulb at a time.

There was no other way to do it. One bulb at a time. No shortcuts. Simply loving the slow process of making it happen, loving the work as it unfolded. Loving an achievement that grew so slowly and that bloomed for only three weeks of each year. Yet, just planting one bulb at a time, year after year, had changed the world.

This unknown woman had forever changed the world in which she lives. She had created something of ineffable magnificence, beauty and inspiration. The principle her daffodil garden taught is one of the greatest principles of celebration: learning to move toward our goals and desires one step at a time - often just one baby step at a time - learning to love the doing, learning to use the accumulation of time.

When we multiply tiny pieces of time with small increments of daily effort, we too will find we can accomplish magnificent things. We can change the world!

As we left the haven of daffodils on the top of that mountain, our minds and hearts were still bathed and bemused by the splendors we had seen. My daughter commented, 'It's as though that remarkable woman has needle-pointed the earth and decorated it. Just think of it, she planted every single bulb for more than 30 years. One bulb at a time! And that's the only way this garden could be created. Every individual bulb had to be planted. There was no way of short-circuiting that process.'

The thought of it filled my mind. I was suddenly overwhelmed with the implications of what I had seen. I felt sad as I thought of what I might have accomplished if I had started toward a goal 35 years ago and had continued working on it all that time. Just think what I might have been able to achieve. As I shared my thoughts with my daughter she simply said, 'Start tomorrow.'

It is pointless to think of the lost hours of yesterdays. The way to make learning a lesson a celebration instead of a cause for regret is to only ask, 'How can I put this to use tomorrow?'"

- Jaroldeen Asplund Edwards

BrightShinyDay@insightoftheday.com

And so it is...

The depth, wonder, power and brilliance of your love is not only
more than you know, it is more than you could
ever possibly imagine."

- Richard Gordon, author of Quantum Touch

Review

1. We often put up blocks for things that will be wonderful.

2. Seeing the magnificent beauty of God's creation
is empowering and inspiring.

3. No matter what goal we have, it requires taking
one little step at a time.

4. It's never too late to begin focusing on your purpose.

Empowerment Activity

Select a dream you have had, no matter how much of a fantasy
it seems it is, and write a paragraph about what your life would
look like if you create that dream into reality.

_____

_____

_____

_____

_____

_____

_____

_____

Affirmation

I choose to begin on my divine path today.

We were born with boundlessness,
the power of God within;
we need only remember.

- Carolyn Porter

12

Remembering Your Power

Part 1

*O*ur birthright is empowerment. We are one with God, the all-powerful energy force of the entire universe, our creator. Being one with God allows this power to be available to us any time we desire it; all we need do is remember it.

We hear these words and on some level we think we have power because that's what we've been told. But we live our life as if we are powerless beings because it's head knowledge, not heart knowledge. And yet we have unlimited possibilities at our fingertips every minute of the day.

I always think of the ocean as a magnificent example of power. The ocean is made of many billions of water droplets. We've seen the power of the ocean as it brings in tides, or waves crash over the beach. Take a cup of water from the ocean and hold it in your hand. In that cup is the fullness of the ocean. Does that cup of ocean water hold the power to bring in the tide? Of course not, but if you throw it back into the ocean where the source of power is, it reconnects and becomes part of the power to bring in a tide.

That's how it is with each one of us. Alone we are powerless, but when we connect to the all-powerful source of Universal Energy, we can do *anything*! All we need to do is to remember to connect!

But most of us allow everyone and everything imaginable to control our lives, rendering us powerless. We are stuck in our "box" where we feel safe and secure because we're afraid to move out of it and grab our power. It's much easier to allow others to take charge of your life and dictate the rules for living it. And if we grabbed our power what would we do with it? That would put us in a place that would frighten most individuals because of the lack of love and self-worth they feel for themselves.

Although every chapter is important in this book and is part of becoming a woman of realness, this chapter stands on its own. I have presented seminars from this chapter and have produced an audio program based on it because of the relevant necessity of understanding this aspect of living in your power.

What exactly is power? According to Webster's New World Dictionary, power is strength, energy, authority, produces an effect, gives the ability to act and is able to influence. Power is authenticity, or realness. So let's discuss each characteristic of power so we better understand the effect it has for empowering our lives. Since this book is about your realness, it's imperative that you comprehend your own power.

Characteristics of Power

Strength

When I mention strength, most people immediately think of physical strength - how strong are you, how big are your muscles, how much can you lift? Physical strength, while certainly a good asset to have, is not the type strength in reference to power. It is inner strength, the courage and determination that enables an individual to move right through the difficult challenges that confront them at times. Maybe you've faced a debilitating or life-threatening disease but made the decision that you weren't going to accept the doctor's diagnosis, so you set out to regain your health. As you accepted the challenge and worked through it, you developed an unbelievable strength of character that you didn't have before. You grew and expanded past the physical illness, and you claimed your power by moving to the other side of the disease. It's the difference between resigning yourself to probable defeat or fighting to the finish for your very breath, whatever the outcome. Arnold Schwartzenegger once said,

> "Strength does not come from winning. Your struggles develop your strength. When you go through hardship and decide not to surrender to it, that is strength."

We have problems in our lives every day and we will as long as we are experiencing this life, but our strength of character is indicated according to our response to the problems. Do we feel like victims and pour loads of self-pity upon ourselves? Do we complain and keep asking God why we are having these problems? Are we assuming that this is just the way life is and succumbing to it? What if, as the problems popped into our lives, we asked for more capabilities to handle the problems, or better yet, asked for a solution to move out of the situation? Doesn't that change the whole perspective of the situation? It may start as a negative event, but if we realize it is a gift for us to become stronger and grow past it, then it's a positive force. When it becomes a positive energy emanating from us, the universe responds as a mirror by reflecting back the same positiveness.

Energy

What is energy? Energy is the inner force that makes things happen. Once energy is created it can never be destroyed. It can change form, but it is always present. Everything in the universe is energy. Our thoughts are energy and every single thought we have creates our life as we see it.

We have over 60,000 thoughts a day and the majority of them are negative. We wonder why things are the way they are in our lives when all along we created it! So we have to take responsibility to make the changes we want in our lives because wherever our energy goes, that's where our power flows. When we focus on our problems they just expand and get bigger. But if we instead focus on the wonderful things we already have, they expand. Which would you rather have expand? Caroline Myss said "All our thoughts, regardless of content, first enter our systems as energy."

One of our biggest problems today is our core belief of lack. Many of us were raised with the thought consciousness that we aren't good enough, we never have enough, and probably don't deserve abundance. Our thoughts are always on our wants - when we get more money, a dream partner, a better job, a larger house, better health or whatever, then we'll be content or happy. So we're always creating lack in our life because that's where our thoughts are. Remember, what we focus on expands.

So it's obvious that energy is a characteristic of power and that whatever we concentrate our thoughts on gets the power. We have a choice to create what we want - abundance or lack. Pay attention to your thoughts each day and you'll be amazed at how many negative thoughts you have. It's been said that the majority of those 60,000 daily thoughts are repeated the next day, so if the majority of them are negative, well, you get the picture.

Authority

When we think of authority, we probably think of someone in charge. Our thoughts go to authority figures such as a policeman, a president, a principal or perhaps our parents. We offer respect to them from our hearts or as a requirement. They portray a command post in the hierarchy of the business they represent. They are leaders and have the power to give orders and make things happen. That is *outside authority*.

The authority that represents a characteristic of power is the authority we have by being one with God. We are given authority over our lives because we are one with God and the authority is already within us and is us. We relinquish our earthly *outside authority* as we tap into divine authority that's already there. This authority is an inborn power and confidence because we are in alignment with God's will. This type of inborn authority actually keeps us humble. We are leaders, not by the force of fear, but out of love, being one with divine love.

Think of an electrical outlet. The energy is there all the time, but until we plug in the radio we can't turn it on and hear the music. It takes us connecting to the source of the energy that gives us the authority (power) to make it happen.

Producing an Effect

Most people spend their lives being the effect of something. They believe things happen and they have no control over them. They are resigned to live the same way because they don't realize they have the power to change it. They are not living causatively.

A man has lived from paycheck to paycheck all of his life. His parents lived that way and his friends all seem to be in the same place financially, so he just assumes that's the way it is: the American way of life. With those thoughts he is the effect of his life.

But let's suppose he decides he wants to change his way of living. He's tired of not having extra money or paying the finance charge on his credit cards. He decides to create a plan to get out of debt and take control of his finances and live within his means. Once he takes the first step into change, he has grabbed his power back and has become causative. All it takes to become causative is to step out of your old patterns into a new consciousness. You are taking action, and action brings results. Your energy has shifted and since you are focusing on a positive you are making a positive change.

Decision + Action = Results

Ability to Act

This characteristic of power invites a person into willingness. Many people have the ability to perform a task, but lack the desire to move forward, usually from fear. Every day as I begin my day with prayer and meditation, I once again say that I am willing to move in whatever direction is for my highest and best as well as that of others. It's not enough to know about your ability; it takes *mobility* from a serving heart.

We see here the issue of low self-worth once again. If we doubt our capabilities we stay where we are. It's a good idea to ask for the capabilities to move forward as well. I often ask for the capabilities to get through whatever circumstances are in my path rather than to take away the situation. This places me in a powerful state as I am willing to gain strength through whatever place I must pass through. When coming from this place you have claimed your power through surrender.

I heard this phrase once and it has remained imbedded in my

memory because of not only the truth in it, but also the power in the words. "Great things are accomplished when you believe that what's inside of you is superior to your circumstances." And to what is this a reference? Power! This of course wipes out the low self-worth concept.

So why not decide right now to erase those old beliefs about your inferiority and replace them with your divine power, knowing that you can accomplish anything. I often use the phrase, "If you see it and believe it, you can achieve it." In my experience, it's always true.

Able to Influence

How would you characterize an influential person? We discussed earlier a leader or person with external authority, an authority figure. Perhaps they can influence you because they hold a position over you. The policeman who gives you a ticket for speeding is just such a person. He dramatically influences you because of the authority he has to affect your life if you don't obey the law.

The influence of a powerful person is an inborn quality. They have the ability to influence people because they are coming from a place of love. You've probably known people like this. They enter a room and you feel their presence, their power. It projects out from them from an inside power, not from some position of leadership or authority. They attract respect and admiration like a magnet because they offer genuineness. This realness from their space of divine power allows you to trust them. They come from a humble heart so their ability to influence you and others shows no competitiveness or manipulative behavior. In fact, it isn't something they even attempt to make happen. It is something that occurs naturally because of internal divine power.

You have probably met individuals who seem powerful because of their ability to influence, perhaps through learned behavioral patterns of manipulation. They may have the ability to draw people to them, but sooner or later they are found out and can no longer hold the attraction. The magnetism is broken because the lack of realness becomes evident.

As I looked back over my life a while ago, I realized my pattern of giving away my power. Parental control was always strongly evident, then a marriage without nurturing that kept me in wanting, then a business partnership that although I grew a great deal during this time, I was kept from knowing my full potential and utilizing it. I began to see the pattern and I knew I had to move onto my own path and live my passion, not someone else's. As I left these experiences in the dust, I felt my power surge through me. But I still found myself doubting all I could do because of my fears and old programming.

One of the hardest aspects for me was going it alone. All my life I'd been part of another's life and I had an identity with that person. As I found myself totally on my own for the first time in my life and in a place of starting over in every way, it was quite scary. I didn't feel powerful, but in hindsight it was a great gift. I was being forced into my power when I stood up for my truth and integrity and followed my own passion. I made a decision to surrender my will and proceed on my path under divine guidance. It was a stepwise progression of events that continually moved me further into my power. Although I still experienced moments of doubt and fear, they gradually became less and less, and I became aware of my self-sabotaging attempts much quicker and was able to let go of them.

So I set out to find answers. What is it that helps people understand their power and reclaim it? What can help me bring my power into reality and help others to do the same? You see, I realized that it wasn't just me who had allowed others to control my life, but that so many people were doing the same thing. So if I could find answers for myself, I could in turn share my insights and alter the life experience for many.

I prayed for guidance and asked for the answer. It came. I received 13 spiritual power tools that enable an individual to grab back their power that's already within them. I smiled when I realized there were 13 tools because 13 is the number that recognizes power. Each one of them is equally vital to the process of becoming powerful, but even incorporating a couple of these tools into your life will create major positive changes for you. When I present this information in a seminar, I always ask the audience to write down ten wonderful things about themselves - abilities, values, gifts - all internal qualities. To depend on the world to validate your self-worth is a no-win expectation. Sometimes people can't think of ten things and often hesitate as they write. This goes back to the low self-worth issue that so many are inflicted with, so I feel that the importance of validating my attendees cannot be overstated.

Some of the 13 tools of empowerment have been discussed in earlier chapters, so they will be only mentioned briefly in this section.

13 Spiritual Power Tools
Part 2

Gratitude
De-powering energy: lack

The most powerful tool according to my guidance is gratitude. Anything other than gratitude comes from lack which is simply fear. I've addressed the "not enough concept" all through this book because it's the base of so many people's life philosophy. Coming from a space of gratitude shifts everything in your belief system and then your life.

If you begin right where you are and realize the bounty you already have and how blessed you really are at this moment, you might be able to see how there is really no lack in your life. You may have *wants,* but there is no lack. The lack is likely your perception of what you want. Granted there may be bills you need to pay or other obligations that should be met, but that's where God comes in. There is nothing unknown to the Higher Power of this universe; all that is unknown to us is the how and the timing. Through faith and surrender, and by you completely turning it over, miracles happen. They may come in another form than you imagined, but they'll come. Not once in my entire life has God ever let me down. Not once when I needed additional funds for a necessity did they not show up. Every time they were there, in some form, and that's a pretty good track record in my book. I'd be willing to bet they've always shown up for you as well.

It's funny how we believe we need so much. We justify this with our perception of what we should have in our life. Often it makes us fall prey to the American way of life: spend. We think we need this and that to "fit in" with everyone else, and if we don't have this or that we are lacking. I used to love to shop. With five children I prided myself on dressing them to the tee from discount places and my own seamstress capabilities. I was an excellent shopper and an excellent seamstress, but I rationalized buying or making more than we really needed because I was able to save so much. I really did save a great deal of money compared to what it would have cost if I didn't make it or get bargains, but we really didn't need all that I purchased or made. One time, when my youngest two daughters were beginning elementary school, I decided to sell all their baby and toddler clothes. I had purchased many expensive, frilly brand-name dresses over the years, but all at discounted prices. As I laid them all out in preparation for selling, it hit me how much money I had spent. I thought about what I might have saved for their education, perhaps half of that money over the last five years, in spite of the money I had "saved."

Later, as I shifted my awareness of what is really important in life, I no longer enjoyed the hours of shopping. I enjoy it occasionally when necessary, but now I shop with a definite idea of what is really needed and usually stick to that. I no longer need what I thought I needed before and I'm saving many hours of time as well. It's fun to go out sometimes just for the fun of it and perhaps buy something out of the ordinary, but it's a special treat for me. I can see that the very consciousness of lack I had always known was causing me to feel that I always needed more, but once I shifted into a consciousness of having enough, everything changed.

Remember this important universal law: whatever you focus on expands. Think about your bounty and be grateful from your heart, and that's what you'll create in your life. Melody Beattie, an author of several books that include the following words from *Codependent No More,*

"Gratitude unlocks the fullness of life. It turns what we have into enough and more. It turns denial into acceptance, chaos to order, confusion to clarity. It can turn a meal into a feast, a house into a home, a stranger into a friend. Gratitude makes sense of our past, brings peace for today, and creates a vision for tomorrow."

I believe she has summed up the whole concept beautifully.

If we are always in the mindset of lack we are negative and cannot produce positives in our life. Whatever we have in our heart is reproduced in our life. Knowing that our resources are unlimited offers us a life of serenity and peacefulness. But knowing we are creators means that if we desire to increase our worldly things for good we can. Beginning with thankfulness expands the bounty, and a thankful heart is a loving heart. Love and gratitude are of spirit. Lack and fear are from ego.

What about all those challenges we receive? Even the times when funds are short and we question where the bounty is? *Every challenge is a gift from God!* I didn't always realize this but I see it clearly now. In fact, if something comes my way that seems like an obstacle, I usually smile now and say "Thank you God. What do you want me to learn this time?" Once we see that these "hard times" are what makes us stronger and growing, they become positive experiences that can actually become high points in our lives. Invariably, as you glance back over the experience, you see many gifts, even when the experience is extremely difficult. You might not want to go through it again, but if you learned the lessons you won't have to. If the same situations keep hitting you in the face, you haven't learned what you need to learn yet. Be grateful for the repeated lesson so you can get it!

A tool that has helped me over the years is a simple but powerful one that can start you in the right direction. Every night, before I go to sleep, I write at least five things in a spiral notebook that I am thankful for. It doesn't have to be a fancy gratitude journal as I first began using, it only needs to be a means for recording your gratitude. These five or so things can be a compliment you received that day, or a new person who entered your life. You could be grateful that the sun was shining, that you're alive and healthy, that you were given an opportunity to help someone that day, or a myriad of things that come to your mind. The list could really go on endlessly, but just listing five things sets the mood for positive, peaceful sleep thoughts. Some people begin their day with writing something in their gratitude journal. That's great, too. Whatever works for you. But do write them down: the writing makes it more impactful in your life.

I begin every prayer time with thanksgiving, lots of it. This is how I begin my morning. On a few rare times when I had something unusual happen and I skipped this part of my day, the entire day was messed up. Try it out and see if it works wonders in your day the way it does in mine.

Forgiveness
De-powering energy: blame, anger, victim consciousness

Forgiving someone who has wronged you according to your perception, is one of the hardest things for most humans to do. It is common to want the wrongdoer to suffer or have his fair share of negative circumstances as retaliation. It is especially true in romantic relationships that break apart. There are hurt feelings with scars that usher in feelings of abandonment, rejection, anger, resentment, bitterness and revenge. The thought of forgiving that person is beyond our comprehension, for we think we are justified in our feelings.

The transition of a relationship is a process that involves many steps. They must all be felt and dealt with to release the negative emotions before moving through it. After moving through it comes forgiveness. Forgiving means loving that individual unconditionally and allowing his divinity to shine through. He is of God just as you are, and you need to release the judgment. Judgment is born of fear and cannot stand with love. If you come from love, you can forgive. Mother Teresa said, "If you judge people you have no time to love them."

When you are not forgiving you are playing small. Love expands you and opens you to understanding beyond our human mind. Fear, where lack of forgiveness is bred, keeps us small and contracting. The only way there can be healing is through love. Marianne Williamson stated, "Forgiveness is the absolute key to healing everything."

Anytime there is an ending to a relationship, there tends to be a list of "grievances" that each feels for the other. If these grievances have been accumulating for years, and they most often do, you could end up with quite a pile. This was the case in my marriage. After 32 years of staying together for various reasons, I knew it was time to end it. But I was sick and trying very hard to get well in the physical realm. I had tried many programs for healing and had certainly improved but was far from well. I began seeing a counselor for help in my illness after a suggestion was made by my holistic health practitioner. It was apparent immediately to the counselor that I needed to forgive my husband for all the perceived hurts I'd experienced. It seemed impossible to do, but I began to ask for God's help as I released the anger. A miracle occurred. As I released the anger and prayed for help in forgiving him, my health soared within a few short weeks.

By the time I filed for divorce, I had literally grown past it and no longer felt anger. I was determined to remain friends since we shared five living children and two in heaven. We are friends and I expect it to remain this way. I learned that physical illness is usually propagated from emotional "baggage," and because of that experience I was able to write my first book *A Woman's Path to Wholeness: The Gift is in the Process*. The book discusses how the baggage keeps us stuck in a box of our own creation and produces a life of fear and need. It goes further by saying that we can choose to move out of the box and create the life we really want. Then we look at our experience as a gift because it helped us grow into a new awareness of life and love. The healing took place as I forgave, allowing me to grow past the external grievances that really didn't matter. *I learned that true forgiveness happens when you no longer feel the need for restitution; the "attachment" was gone.* I was free from the bondage of that anger and the list of grievances, and it was wonderful. I had been able to go beyond human understanding of love and see firsthand what real divine love is.

But there was another person to forgive that I hadn't yet - myself. It was many months later when I became aware that even though I thought I had forgiven my husband, I couldn't understand fully the realm of forgiveness until I forgave myself. My true healing came when I understood the core of my healing involved self-forgiveness. I kept hanging onto my negative beliefs about myself - low self-esteem, defective, incapable, guilty, undeserving - all directed at me. The process showed up after working through many programs of self-realization and release and trying to find someone to fix me. One day it hit me, as if I just turned the light switch on, that I had to do the work myself. I had to recognize the limiting patterns and the old set of shackles that were keeping me in the same circumstances. I realized I had to set myself free by forgiving myself and moving past it all. I was my own worst judge and jury and it was time to remove myself from that courtroom. No longer did I feel the need to punish myself for the "errors" of my past. I felt compassion for myself and understood that everything had presented itself in my life so I could learn from it. A burden was lifted when I realized that self-condemnation was over.

Learning to forgive by releasing all the branches of fear from lack of forgiveness - bitterness, resentment, anger, revenge, victim - is an extremely powerful tool of empowerment. Seeing the situation from the other person's viewpoint is also empowering. Look at the one who hurt you as a wounded spirit. You don't have to agree with what they did or said, but sending love with forgiveness and then detaching from the emotion of the relationship frees you because it diffuses the emotion surrounding the situation. Apply this to your self-forgiveness and free yourself. Create a new script for your life, one that sees you perfect and loving with unlimited possibilities and capabilities.

Value Yourself
De-powering energy: low self-worth

Valuing yourself has been the main theme of this book. Knowing your own worth with all the ramifications that implies is what every one of you must comprehend to become a woman of realness. As I've said so many times already, God created us in perfection and therefore we have the birthright of worthiness. As we own our brilliance we open up for greater abundance and vitality to enter our lives.

When you know your own worth you feel confident in life experiences. You know it's your journey and no one else has anything to do with your self-value. Being one with God you already have everything at your disposal, and all you must do is connect with the all-powerful force of the universe to create it in your life. The value we place with ourselves is what we project to the world. What shows up in our life is in direct relationship to what we believe internally. Defectiveness and unworthiness bring problems, lack and all kinds of self-reproach, but believing in ourselves as a valuable work of art brings the desired good into our lives.

Living on Purpose
De-powering energy: no passion

This has been discussed in the chapter entitled Stepping Into Your Passion in great detail. Knowing what ignites your internal fire is what brings into your life the fulfillment and happiness for which you are searching. As you live your passion and extend it outward to the world, you become a powerful servant of love. There is nothing greater in this world than to know you are serving others with your purpose. You become a rock on which the foundation of your life and the work you are doing is built. It takes courage as you step out in faith, but you will become a stronghold of endurance and capabilities as you proceed on your journey called life. Your life will exude enthusiasm. Enthusiasm simply means God within us.

Allowing God to Flow Through
De-powering energy: control

Letting go of our control is often one of the hardest things an individual has to do. We want to control all that we can because we believe that controlling makes us powerful. In actuality, the control makes us weak and causes great stress as we continually seek the perceived power of the control.

Many people are weak and allow this kind of behavior to occur. They would rather just give in than oppose, feeling this leads to peacefulness. It may make this person feel better as they attempt to please the other person, but this behavior is a kind of codependency, or addiction, that results in losing control.

I've alluded to the importance of surrender many times already. Surrender is the way we gain our power but most people don't see that. Giving up control makes people feel lesser and weaker, so they grab onto the control any way they can. A person addicted to alcohol feels better when they drink, but as it wears off they go into depression and perhaps aggressive behavior because they hate themselves. But in the power of the effects of substance abuse they are disillusioned into believing they are powerful. At the base of it all is low self-esteem. Their attempt at control to build themselves up backfires as they succumb to the destructive effects of the alcohol. The only way this individual can ever release the addiction is in surrender.

As you give up your own control of situations and individuals you claim your power. In so doing you are empowering others.

Wayne Dyer says, "Authentic power is the ability to empower others; you give up control." In the case of someone who is addicted to alcohol, if you continually cover up and make excuses for their behavior, you are giving away your power to them and the alcohol and both are hiding from life. If on the other hand you decide not to cover up for this person anymore, you are forcing them to confront their problem and are giving them the choice of empowerment, and at the same time are empowering yourself. It all happens in letting go.

As I was about to birth my fifth child, I asked my husband to be part of a natural childbirth. He was not in accord with the idea but I continued to beg and plead; I really wanted him present. Where we lived at that time required a one-time class for the new dad to be invited into the labor room, regardless of how many previous births there had been. In the middle of the class he left and I knew this idea was vanquished. Never after that night did I ever mention it again and I literally let it go. I had birthed four alone and could do it again, and it looked as if this was to be. But an angel appeared as I was about to enter the delivery room in the form of a little blue-haired granny nurse who told him to suit up. He told her he wasn't going in. but she argued with him a few minutes, and to my total disbelief, he was suiting up as I was wheeled into delivery. I had let go of it entirely and it happened. It didn't happen exactly the way I had pictured it, but he was there, which is what I wanted. The way it happened was unimportant!

When we let go and allow God to flow through our desires are brought to us. They may look different than we pictured them, but if they do they will actually look better than our vision. God's power is our power and as we surrender into the will of God we become powerful divine beings.

Honesty
De-powering energy: untruth

An old saying that's been around for eternity it seems is that honesty is the best policy. I agree. Honesty is of God and certainly is based of love. Anything less than truth breeds lack of trust, and I believe, as do many others, that trust and honesty are simultaneous.

If someone tells you an untruth, what does that automatically do in your mind? More than likely you will hesitate believing them the next time they tell you something. Certainly if it occurs several times you quit believing them. What happens when your teenager breaks your trust by staying out past curfew or going someplace you've instructed them not to go? Maybe next time you'll follow them!!! You'll probably have a great deal of doubts for a while until your trust in them rebuilds over time.

Dishonesty immediately de-powers an individual. Linda Larson states in her book *True Power* that trust equals power. A trustworthy person is congruent, which means they "walk their talk." The congruency enhances their credibility which immediately builds trust in that person. A trustworthy person is a powerful person.

If someone preaches to you about health and fitness, telling you to do this and do that to be healthy, but you see them continually stopping by the fast food establishments and downing soft drinks by the case while their midriff continues to expand, are you going to believe them and follow their suggestions? Of course not, because they aren't walking their talk. Business leaders who exhibit questionable behavior will eventually lose ground with those who honor truth. Here is a story that depicts the power of standing in the light of honesty.

Several decades ago a president of a large company called one of his executives in another state and invited him to attend a prestigious luncheon. He would fly him to the luncheon on the company expense account while he dined with the top leaders of the company. The man was overwhelmed and graciously accepted. During the extravagant luncheon the president came to talk with the executive. He mentioned he wanted to make an announcement saying that this executive would be the new executive vice-president of the company and would have a seat on the Board. The executive was flabbergasted but readily agreed and promised to uphold the standards of the company and continue to promote the company in every way possible. The president said he was glad the executive had said that and went on to say he was expected to always vote however the president told him to vote. A red flag went up for the executive and as the conversation continued and he raised objections, he realized he had to refuse the offer. Furthermore, the more they discussed the situation the more the executive realized he couldn't be part of this company in any way. He couldn't be part of unethical behavior, and not standing for his own truth would be unethical. He resigned on the spot and left.

He was devastated. He had a family and wasn't sure what would happen next, but he knew he had to walk his talk and stand in his truth no matter what. Several evenings later, as he was sitting in his home, a knock came on the door. Opening the door revealed six of the executives standing there from the company he had left. The spokesman said they had heard how he stood up for truth and they were proud of him. They also had resigned their jobs and had come to support him by working with him. Those seven men sat at his table that night and created his new company. It was a company built on honesty and it became a large empire. What appeared to be a bad situation when the executive walked away with no job, ended up being much more than what he had left, because he stood for honesty and integrity.

Honesty is always the best policy! If you cheat someone or are deceptive it will come back to grab you eventually. It's the universal law of cause and effect. But remember to be honest with yourself, which is the key to your true freedom.

Listening to Your Inspiration
De-powering energy: listening to others

So often in our lives we listen to everyone else, allowing them to dictate our beliefs. To be powerful we need to listen to our own thoughts and insights. We do need to be careful as we can lose our perspective at times, but we must go in to find our own beliefs instead of listening to everyone else's. When we listen to others we are taking on their model of the world, not ours.

I'm not saying we should never absorb into our being the insights of others because many times they are valuable, as long as they support our growth and enhance our purpose. Anything less than that doesn't serve us and must be discarded. So often our friends and family discourage us the most because they try to make us believe they have our best interests at heart, but they really have *their* own interests at heart.

Remember that our thoughts are energy so once created they are broadcast out to the world. They cannot be taken back and are continually circulating the vibration of what we created. If they are negative they latch onto other negativity and build momentum, adding more negativity. On the other hand, if they're positive loving thoughts, they reap more love as they spread those cosmic waves. Every thought is an energy vibration that mirrors back to us. Knowing this should make us mindful of what we are thinking, saying and doing.

Affirmations - positive statements verbalized out loud in the present - can assist the process of changing your thoughts. An example might be: "I am a powerful woman who stands in my own truth," or "I am a powerful woman who can do anything I want to do without limitations." Both of these can powerfully assist reprogramming your belief system and should be stated repeatedly throughout the day. Even if you don't believe it at the onset, saying it over and over can change your inner beliefs, thoughts, words and actions.

Decision
De-powering energy: procrastination

Do you know what procrastination really is? Self-sabotage! That's right. If you continually put things off your ego is working overtime and having a field day!

Procrastination is simply a form of fear. We procrastinate when we're afraid to do something we don't understand or don't want to do. If you put it off you don't have to make a decision. We so often sit on the proverbial fence of indecision, one foot in the old door as we try desperately to hold on in case the new door isn't to our liking; we're afraid to take that leap. But it's not possible to have one foot in each door; as long as we remain there we go nowhere.

Decision gives us power. We have made a choice and now must move forward with our choice. This involves action - taking steps to make it happen. It is at this point that we set goals. Goals are simply daydreams with a deadline. Without the deadline we often don't fulfill the dream. How many times have you made those New Years resolutions that never happen? How many times have you said you are going to start an exercise program and take off those extra 20 pounds? How about that book you planned to start five years ago and is still in your head? Something else always takes your time and the program is never begun. However, when you put a date to it you create accountability. The date psychologically tells your mind there is a time-frame in which this must be accomplished. Of course you can always choose not to fulfill the goal, but more often it will be accomplished with a date attached. Successful people set goals and achieve them. Once the universe sees you're serious about achieving this goal, the universe steps in with assistance.

Now envision what you want. What do you see for your life? What do you wish to achieve? What job, relationship, lifestyle, wealth accumulation is in your vision? How do you see yourself serving others? Once you create your vision you want to make it come alive, and you do this with feeling. The more emotion you put into your dream the faster it will manifest in your life. Use the senses: sight, sound, smell, taste, touch and intuition. The more feeling the more alive it is. Do you want to open your own business? See the building, what your office looks like and hear the people talking around you. What color schemes are in the offices, how do you feel, what do your clothes look like, can you smell the coffee brewing, who are your clients or customers, and so on. Do this daily and watch what happens.

The *feeling* of the vision is what makes it come alive but all the feeling in the world will not make it happen. You must add *action* and take the steps necessary. So many times we begin those steps but a challenge pops in out of the blue and stops us in our tracks. You can be sure as soon as you make a decision to move forward in a new direction your ego will also make a decision - to block you. Obstacles will appear right in front of you before you take your second step, so you must focus, never taking your eyes off of your goal. Why does your ego do this? Because the ego is a control freak and wants you to continue just as you have been with the ego in control of your life through fear. That's the only way it can survive, and if you begin a new path the ego loses ground rapidly. To prevent that from happening it puts up a powerful fight. This is why you can never take your eyes off of your goal. If you do you may never get back on track, and you may leave this planet having never achieved what you could have done. A statement I read once from a daily email motivational service went like this: "Most of your obstacles would melt away if, instead of cowering before them or procrastinating about dealing with them, you would make up your mind to walk boldly through them. The attainment of your dreams is but a determined action away." I believe that says it all.

Validating Others
De-powering energy: ego

Earlier we talked about validating yourself and recognizing your own worth. While that must come before you can see other people's worth, it is important to recognize them. It's easy sometimes to get so wrapped up in our ego's selfish messages that we forget how important other people are. Failing to acknowledge their worth takes away our power. How many times have we heard someone say they wished they had told that relative or friend what they meant to them before they left this planet? Make it a point every day to share your feelings with those you love, which of course should be everyone! Send a note, call them on the phone, stop by and visit, or whatever allows you to share your love with them, validating them.

Every person on this planet is part of God, which makes them part of you. It doesn't matter what the color of their skin is, whether you like them or not, or whether you've ever met them. You are connected to them. Since they are part of you it makes sense to recognize their worth, for in essence you are recognizing yourself.

Show appreciation for things people do for you. Be free with the words, "Thank you." Give *genuine* compliments and let them feel good about themselves through you. Acknowledge their gifts and talents. Help them in every way you can. Zig Ziglar said, "Help others get what they want and you will get what you want." This is so true. Remember the pebble in the pond? The ripples that go out also come back to you. Often you will find many more blessings in the compliments you give to others than the ones that come to you.

No Fear
De-powering energy: being stuck

Since we worked through fear earlier it isn't necessary to go through it again. Just remember that living in fear renders you powerless, giving the power to the fear. A quote I often use in talks I give goes like this: "He who is afraid of a thing gives it power over him." Love is where the power is!

Living Today
De-powering energy: living in the past or future

In the chapter entitled Just Be we discussed the importance of living in the present. Past regrets do not make us powerful but rather defeat us. The future isn't here yet so we cannot experience it. Living in the anticipation of something we expect also takes away our power. The only space in which we experience power is in the now. We live in the present.

Time Management
De-powering energy: non-organization

Successful people utilize time that unsuccessful people waste. That's a powerful statement. Someone who is organized is much more productive because they use time wisely. They know how to systemize their life and insert time for fun and relaxation if they choose. By managing their time they remove the chaos that so many people experience daily.

There are 168 hours in every week. The average person wastes at least three hours per day, making a total of at least 21 hours per week. That's a lot of hours that could have been put to better use. Some people waste many more hours than that and they will never be as successful as one who manages their time.

So how do you mange your time efficiently? One of the most valuable tools I've ever encountered is a Things To Do List. Every day I write down what I must accomplish that day - errands, appointments, tasks, phone calls - anything that needs to be done. As I complete them I check them off. Anything not accomplished is added to the next day or whatever day is appropriate. I never leave home without my list. As a result I remember what I need to do, and by keeping track of my responsibilities it makes my life run much smoother. I am normally very organized, but being human with a lot on my mind, it's easy to become forgetful at times. My list keeps me on track.

With lack of organization we find clutter. Clutter predisposes confusion which is in opposition to power. Taking charge of your time and sticking to your schedule can actually free up more time for you to play. One of my sons and I (and I have his permission to say this!) were having a discussion about time management a few months ago. We were talking about the things to do list and how valuable it is. When he responded unwittingly, "I'm so unorganized I don't have time to be organized," we had one of those treasured moments of laughter when we realized what he had said. But isn't that how many people view it? I feel it shows responsible behavior when you become organized and a custodian of your time. A powerful person manages her time and is therefore productive.

Work to Please You
De-powering energy: being a people pleaser

So many people spend their entire lives saying yes to everyone but themselves. Life to them is about pleasing everyone else. They have no idea who they are because their lives are run by their parents, spouse, children, employer, family or friends. This is a powerless person.

You can't live anyone else's life and they can't live yours, no matter how hard either of you try. But many people allow others to think for them. In order to be powerful it is imperative to stand on your own two feet and set your own boundaries. That might mean saying no at times because it's not in your best interest, even if the other person gets upset.

You probably have a very long list of times when you said "yes" when you really wanted to say "no." We've all been there, some of us more than others, sucking up as we give in. We've done this for various reasons, but it all stems from fear. Were we trying to keep a job or get a promotion, hang onto a relationship, win favors, be accepted, be loved, gain a position, acquire wealth, or dozens of other things? Every one of these has a base in resistance, attachment, codependency, busyness, greed, low self-worth - in other words, fear.

A powerful individual sets boundaries. They learn to say no because they set limits for certain things that overload them. This is not the same as limiting our potentiality, which is doing for everyone else instead of ourselves. Our primary function in this life is to follow our purpose, not anyone else's purpose. If we continually overcommit to projects that are not our purpose, then our work is limited. That's not to say we shouldn't ever contribute to projects that other people initiate because as a collective body we need to help each other, but it must not interfere with the work that we are here to do.

Most of the time, when people sign up to help everyone else instead of doing their own purpose, it's a self-sabotaging tactic. If they're so busy, even doing spiritual projects, then there isn't time to proceed down their path. They justify it as noble and honorable work, which of course it is, but it's a cover up for their own fear of moving ahead on their journey. Our ego is so sneaky, a real con artist, and manipulates our minds to believing our sabotaging thoughts.

A good way to decide if something is worthy of your time at that particular moment, is to ask yourself if doing this will further your purpose. For several years I worked very hard for someone else's purpose. I sabotaged myself into believing this was where I was to be. I learned a great deal and certainly reaped valuable lessons, but when I didn't figure it out on my own the old cosmic two-by-four whacked me and got my attention. As I looked back on those years I recognized the pattern of pleasing others at my own expense and realized it was a pattern of a lifetime. I vowed right then that this pattern was over. As I began focusing my energy into my purpose amazing things unfolded. This book is one of them. Although being a team player can be a worthy endeavor, make sure it is part of your purpose and not an excuse to put yours on the back burner.

These tools can be powerful adjuncts in helping you claim your power. A powerful person is connected to God and can do anything - no limits. We are here to give back to the world from our bounty that is within us. *Everything else takes second place.* Begin today to put to use these power tools of empowerment. Understand that it's a step by step process. Begin simply with a tool or two and as you implement them into your life you'll experience a surge of power. Then add another tool and feel the surge again. Sometimes you'll slip back into old ways. Don't beat yourself up. Recognize where you are and simply take another step forward. The more you use these tools the more powerful you'll become. All you are doing as you claim your power is remembering that it's already inside you!

"You are capable of doing something absolutely incredible with your life. The same power that runs through "stars" also runs through you!"

- Bob Proctor, author of You Were Born Rich

Review

1. Our birthright is empowerment.
Our power is already within us. All we need do is remember it.

2. We need to understand what power is.
*The following are characteristics of power: strength, energy,
authority, producing an effect, the ability to act,
and being able to influence.*

3. There are thirteen spiritual power tools.
1. Gratitude
2. Forgiveness
3. Value yourself
4. Living on purpose
5. Allowing God to flow through
6. Honesty
7. Listening to your inspiration
8. Decision
9. Validating others
10. No fear
11. Living today
12. Time management
13. Working to please you

Empowerment Activity

How many pertain to you? Each one you check demonstrates a
way in which you give your power away.

___ Buy things to impress   ___ Are holding a grudge

___ Are a pleaser   ___ Relive past pain

___ Procrastinate   ___ Often late

___ Exaggerate the truth   ___ Worry

___ Manipulate to get your way   ___ Feel "stuck"

___ Work mainly for a paycheck   ___ Feel like a doormat

___ Say "yes" but mean "no"   ___ Are critical of others

___ Love to talk about yourself ___ Daydream but no action

___ Frequently apologize about yourself

___ Know you shouldn't do it but do

___ Live paycheck to paycheck

___ Need to be in a relationship

Affirmation

*I choose to claim my power and not
yield to the control of others.*

A baby's cry, a sweet little kiss,
A wink, a smile, a warm embrace,
A flower blooms, raindrops fall,
The sun glistens on our face.
It's a miracle.

Stars twinkling right through the night
As the wind whispers in our ear,
Snowflakes drift gracefully down from above,
In silence blanketing both far and near.
It's a miracle.

The sea, majestic, its power unmatched
Both turbulent and peaceful can be,
The mighty oak but an acorn was once,
Such wonders, so amazing we see.
It's a miracle.

Challenges do come and line our path
Breaking our spirit it seems,
But stronger are we, growing, expanding,
Rising, to follow our dreams.
It's a miracle.

How blessed are our lives, grateful we be
For our gifts that oft come so disguised,
Every breath, every moment, every memory in time
Blessings of life shining forth to our eyes.
It's a miracle.

We only need ask, the miracles are there
Just barely beyond our reach,
So believe, keep your faith, hold open your hands
And grasp God's abundance for to keep.
Always believe in miracles!

                                        - Carolyn Porter

13

Coincidence or Miracle?

*I*n my awareness there are no coincidences. I am convinced that every experience of unexplained happenstance is another small miracle. Your beliefs may be different, but I accept the multiple times that rather strange and extraordinary things popped into my life's viewing were simply God showing up with tiny miracles, and sometimes big ones. I'll share one such happening that continues to "blow my mind"!

Earlier in the year of this writing I enjoyed my first TV appearance on a 30-minute live show. Since the show was a two-hour drive from my home, I decided to make good use of the trip by scheduling two book-signings at big book chains in the city. I was doing the second book-signing when a man came up to my table. He asked a few questions, looked at my book then put it down, but gave me his business card indicating that he was a radio producer. He said if I came back to the area to call him and he'd try to get me on the air. I put his card in my card file once I got home and didn't think of it until…

About a month later I had been out doing errands and walked into my bedroom, noticing a card lying in the middle of my floor. I picked it up wondering why it was there because I hadn't been into my card file that's in my office (another room), and in fact hadn't been home since early morning. I laid it on my desk and wondered where it came from and why it was there. Three days later I received an email from this man named on the card, sharing with me that he was writing a book and asked if I would read the first chapter and give my opinion. I was delighted to do this for him and promptly shared with him that I was presenting a seminar on writing and self-publishing shortly and suggested he attend. He signed up the next day, even though it would require him to drive a considerable distance. But he shared something even more incredible. He said the only reason he was in the bookstore when I was doing the signing was for a cup of coffee. Starbucks is in the bookstore and because the coffee was in the process of completion, he had walked over to my table. Coincidence or miracle?

But the story continues. He has since connected me with two great people in other states who have connections that are in the process of getting me into new places. Not only that, he has become a wonderful friend. Recently he connected me with someone else in the same city who has led me to other places and new people with seminars and events all in the making. And to think it all began with a man wanting a cup of freshly brewed coffee!!! So was it a coincidence or miracle? How did that card find a place on my floor without my physical assistance just days before he became an important part of my life with a continuous stream of new connections!

How about the person that is driving on the expressway and

misses the exit that he knows he's supposed to take but his mind has wandered. Then he hears later about a terrible accident that occurred on that exit about the time he would have been traveling there. Could it be an angelic miracle? We all have many stories like this with unexplainable interference that shows up as protection when we look back on it.

Sometimes things happen that seem to hurt us but later we find have been a precious gift. A woman had just lost her mother, her friend. The daughter was grieving, sitting in the church barely listening to the minister as her mind stretched out over years of memories. She sat alone as her brother sat with his wife and children and her sister leaned against her husband. Suddenly she heard the church door open and hurrying footsteps came right to where she was sitting. A man sat down next to her, his eyes brimming with tears as he said softly "I'm late." After a few eulogies he leaned over to the woman and asked "Why do they keep referring to the deceased as Mary since her name was Margaret? The woman replied "Her name was Mary Peters." So the man asked "Is this the Lutheran church" to which the woman answered "No, that church is across the street. I believe you're at the wrong funeral, Sir."

The solemnness of the occasion mixed with the realization of the man's mistake bubbled up inside the woman and came out as laughter. She cupped her hands over her face hoping it would be interpreted as sobs. But the creaking pew gave her away. The mourners commenced to shoot sharp looks at her which only made the situation worse. In bewilderment she glanced at the man who was now laughing too. It was too late for an uneventful exit as she imagined her mother looking in and laughing with them. As soon as they could the woman and the man escaped to the parking lot where they took a deep breath and began talking about what had happened. The man had missed his aunt's funeral in this mix-up, but since you can never return to what has passed, they decided to finish the afternoon over a cup of coffee. A year after that funeral experience they were married and at this writing have been together for over 22 years. What began as an assumed "mistake" ended up bringing two people together for a lifelong journey. They jokingly tell people when asked how they met that "Her mother and my aunt Mary introduced us, and it's truly a match made in heaven!" Don't ever underestimate the power of God's miracles, however they show up!

Situations come into our lives that may seem dreadful, like losing your job. Perhaps it's a sign to move in a new direction. I believe that any time a door closes it means you are being protected. It also means that another door is about to open. You might need to exhibit patience, which is often a difficult state to achieve. With this state comes faith and surrender. As you exhibit the art of waiting, the miracles appear.

You've probably heard the saying, "When the student is ready the teacher appears." Would you call the teacher a coincidence? I've had so many situations where in hindsight I see a tremendous gift from a "teacher" who was placed in front of me at just the right time. I'm sure you know what I'm talking about. It might even be an unpleasant situation that wakes you up, forcing you to change and grow. I believe these "teachers" are catalysts used divinely to revive our spirits. They who push our buttons the most are our greatest teachers!

The list of coincidences that are really God's anonymous miracles is endless. As we look out over our lives and see how it is unfolding, we see example after example of these miracles that show up as coincidences. I often glance in awe at the chain of events that has made my life what it is today. Nothing is amiss or out of place. Everything is exactly what it was supposed to be to make this life experience as it is. But just one itsy bitsy decision change would have altered the entire chain of events. And it wouldn't have been wrong or messed up, just a different life experience.

Our miracles come in strange packages sometimes. The gift may be hidden for a long time. It might be after the fact as we glance over all that has occurred that we see how beautifully wrapped this gift was. That happens many times in relationships that move apart. There is so much pain when it happens that you cannot see the gift. But in hindsight you see how the relationship wasn't nurturing your soul any longer and the parting was necessary for your growth. Time allows you to see the gift as a new door opens, taking you into new awareness you wouldn't have had if you remained in the relationship. You were being protected from stagnation.

Many of you have experienced big miracles in your life: a miraculous cure from a serious disease, the sudden healing of a relationship that was broken, a long-awaited pregnancy or a job promotion that frees you from financial bondage. With pride you watch your daughter, a vision in white, float down the aisle on her wedding day or your son as he beams from ear to ear on the first day his new business opens. Every single day of our lives we experience miracles. No matter how insignificant they may seem compared to something as joyous as the healing of a life-threatening illness, each one is just as magnificent as the other.

Sometime, when you have a few moments to sit quietly and look into nature, stop and appreciate all the miracles. An acorn falls to the ground and through a natural chain of events becomes the beautiful oak tree you now see. A butterfly lights on the fence and you realize it used to be a caterpillar but through a chain of miracles is now this beautiful winged creature. You hear the chirping of birds in the tree beyond where you sit and you marvel at how they know just when to sing. The rainbow is glistening in the distance now that the storm has passed. Everywhere you look there are miracles - God at work. Your life is one miracle after another.

All the events that appeared and linked the next step on your path are not coincidences, but are God's miracles. Think of your son or daughter and remember the wonderment of that new life growing inside of you, who perhaps is now all grown up and living their own journey - truly a miracle from God. Not one thing is out of place; not one thing is a coincidence. Every miracle is a seed for a stream of miracles. All we see in every direction far and near are miracles! But the greatest miracle of all is *You!*

"As for me, I know of nothing else but miracles."

- Walt Whitman, American poet

Review

1. Unexplained happenstances are not coincidences,
but God's tiny (or big) miracles.
They show up every day.

∽

2. Every experience has a gift.
When the student is ready the teacher appears as a gift.

∽

3. Appreciate all the miracles in nature and your life.
*We experience big miracles and small miracles,
each one just as significant.*

Empowerment Activity

Make a list of miracles you've experienced in the last 24 hours.

1. _____
2. _____
3. _____
4. _____
5. _____
6. _____
7. _____
8. _____
9. _____
10. _____
11. _____
12. _____

Express gratitude to God for all the miracles you have already experienced and all that are coming to you.

Affirmation

I choose to be grateful for everyone of God's miracles in my life.

Life's answers lie within;
be still and listen to the voice of your spirit
as it speaks softly to you.
Deep within the silence your truth abides;
there is the light that shines
to illumine your path.

- Carolyn Porter

14

Knowing Your Truth

In preparation for writing this book I was guided to take a survey that included the following questions. Although I questioned men and women from ages 18 to 65, I found the answers quite similar. There was basically no difference because of age or sex in what the majority of the answers were.

1. What quality is most important for your partner to have?
2. What is the most important value for yourself?
3. What do you love the most about yourself?
4. What do you dislike the most about yourself?
5. Why do you think most relationships break apart?
6. What is love?

I will reveal the results of all the questions throughout this chapter, but I want to touch on the first one now. The overwhelming majority answer for the first question was honesty. Out of 125 completed surveys, almost 50 % said honesty/ trustworthy was most important. It was the top choice of both men and women of all ages. I thought about that long and hard. What irony! The largest percentage of those surveyed want honesty in their partner above all else. Are they honest with themselves?

We've talked throughout this book about the pebble in the pond effect, how the ripples come back to us eventually. Well, how can you expect to attract honest partners if you aren't honest with yourself? We stay in jobs we don't like, in relationships that don't serve, hang onto old beliefs and patterns that should be discarded, ignore the quiet urges to move forward, hide from our capabilities because of fear, sabotage ourselves into believing we aren't worthy, and as a result push away all the things we really would like in our lives. We often don't even know what our core values are, on what we want to base our life.

What are your base values? What qualities are the foundation on which you are building your life? I've listed some base values that could be significant to your life. Read them and take them in. See which ones resonate with your spirit. Which ones are already incorporated in your system base and which ones need to be utilized as a powerful person?

Honesty	Integrity
Punctuality	Openness
Forgiveness	Compassion
Morality	Gratitude
Appreciation	Encourager
Congruency	Commitment
Perseverance	Completes task
Confidence	Acceptance
Love	Compatibility
Thoughtfulness	Understanding

Sincerity　　　　　*Trust*
Supportive　　　　　*Humility*
Inner Strength　　　*Courage*
Listener　　　　　　*Patience*

Knowing your core values is your foundation. Many people never stop to think about what they value. How long will you stand in your truth before you succumb to external pressure, or will you stand firm at all costs? First you must know what those values are. If you are seeking your realness you have to begin with the foundation. What kind of a life will it be unless it's built on a solid foundation that promotes truth?

A father of a wealthy boy decided to take his young son on a trip to the country with the firm purpose of showing his son how poor people can be. They spent a few days and nights on the farm of what would be considered a very poor family. On their return from their trip the father asked his son how he enjoyed the trip. The son said "It was great, Dad."
"Did you see how poor people can be?" the father asked.
"Oh yeah" said the boy.
"So what did you learn from the trip?" asked the father.
This is what the son replied.
"I saw that we have one dog and they had four. We have a pool that reaches to the middle of our garden and they have a creek that has no end. We have imported lanterns in our garden and they have the stars at night. Our patio reaches to the front yard and they have the whole horizon. We have a small piece of land to live on and they have fields that go beyond our sight. We have servants who serve us, but they serve others. We buy our food, but they grow theirs. We have walls around our property to protect us; they have friends to protect them."

The boy's father was speechless. Too many times we forget what we have and concentrate on what we don't have. One person's worthless object is another's prize possession.

Each of us has much to value in our life at this moment. Where is our focus? Do we really see the valuable treasures or are we trying so hard to accumulate things in this world that we miss what's real? We each have our own model of the world. This is our truth, on which we are building our life. Are your values taken from the previous list or are your values based on tangible things that break, fade, get outdated or lose value? In the story above, who is really the richest?

The second question I asked in the survey is "What quality is the most important quality for yourself?" Here again, honesty, or standing in your own truth, ranked top for all. It seems to me that most people are yearning for truth in themselves as well as others.

When I asked the third question I noticed quite a few people hesitated before answering. Some even said they didn't love anything about themselves. Again I was baffled. Do many people really think they have nothing to love about themselves? If this is true then how in the world do they imagine ever finding a loving partner? And how sad for those who actually said there was nothing they loved about themselves. Although this isn't a representation of the entire population, I feel it's a pretty good representation of the prevailing mindset of the vast majority of society or we wouldn't be battling so much low self-worth and its effects.

And so we have gone full circle regarding low self-worth. We must transform our inner beliefs or our lives will reflect the same situations and experiences. When asking the fourth question - what do you dislike the most about yourself - it only took a second for the person to rattle something off. We have so many grievances against ourselves when we need to accept ourselves unconditionally. In the chapter on acceptance we discussed this in detail. It's time to shift our perceptions to loving ourselves, even the things we want to change. The number one answer here was a tie between their weight and procrastination. Procrastination is simply self-sabotage, born of fear. The weight issue requires changing lifestyle practices and that can be created differently as well. It begins within the individual.

Why do so many relationships break apart? Just about everyone said because of communication problems. Psychologists and marriage counselors have agreed for years that communication is at the root of most marital problems. Even if finances are the biggest issue in divorce, communication is at the core. Communication involves a very important aspect that eludes most people, that of listening. Often, before a person completes what he/she is saying we are ready with a comment or answer. This creates all kinds of communication problems because in our limited perception we have already decided our perception of what is being said without fully listening. The other face of this is the lack of acceptance of the individual as they are. We have our own expectation of how they should be according to our perception, so if they come from a different place we don't accept it. Therefore, communication issues are created. If on the other hand, we take the time to listen to their perception, we might find they have something valuable to say!

Several years ago I heard the story below of a mental and verbal conversation that occurred between a husband and wife. Maybe it didn't cause a break-up of the relationship, but if not resolved over the years, it could precipitate disengagement.

A man came home from a long week of work, thinking how tired he was. He had been asked to play golf the next morning and readily agreed. He thought how much he deserved this relaxing, fun activity and thought how much better he'd be for his family the rest of the weekend if he had some time to play. So he tells his wife that he's playing golf and she shows her displeasure immediately. She's thinking how absent he's been all week and how she didn't have his attention much. She thought he'd want to spend time with her and the kids but instead he wants to play golf. She thinks how selfish he is and that he must not love her very much anymore. Her mind wanders to thoughts that maybe their relationship is winding down and she gets very quiet.

Each partner had a different perception. If they don't communicate their thoughts, there's a serious problem in the making. Neither one was wrong or right, just different. This kind of situation happens again and again in relationships. If we come from the heartspace of love and acceptance these misunderstandings could be eliminated.

The final question I asked on the survey was "What is love?" Many people had to think a minute to decide what love was to them. Many said this was hard. Why would this be hard for so many? Because they don't really know what love is. One young man chuckled when I asked him and I reminded him that the answer would have nothing to do with physical feel-goods. Most people thought immediately of the physical feelings of romantic love, but when they got down to the real meaning of love, they hesitated. The most common answer was caring or trust in the other person. I feel love also must involve acceptance without conditions. In any case, it got most people thinking about things they hadn't thought about for a long time.

It's time for you to know your truth. What is love and how do you create love in your life? What are the core values that are building the foundation of your life as you experience it? Your truth has nothing to do with your parents' beliefs, what your spouse, friends, neighbors, employer, minister or coach believes. It has only to do with you. That petrifies many folks because it means they must take time to think! But until you do this you cannot become real. Standing firm in the knowing of your own realizations is very powerful. Understanding that another's truth may look different than yours is empowering. Letting go of the judgment of their truth frees you into your empowerment.

Cheryl Richardson, author of *Life Makeovers*, says,

> "We all have different sets of internal rules which make up our personal integrity. Most people are unaware of how much energy it takes to live outside of our internal rules. When we restore our integrity we release enormous amounts of energy that can serve our present-day lives."

Wherever our energy goes is where our power is.

My number one value has always been honesty. Nothing breaks my trust in someone faster than untruth. I can remember my parents telling me that once I break trust with them it'll take a long time to rebuild their trust in me. Of course that was rooted in the judgment concept of life, but many people come from this mindset. If we come from non-judgment, we can release the incident and move on. Detachment from this person would probably be necessary since you no longer resonate on the same vibration.

I believe that honesty must be at the base of a powerful person's life. Power is of God. God is love. Love goes hand in hand with honesty. As we discussed earlier, honesty builds trust, which builds congruency and provides credibility. Go inside and know your truth. In the silence your truth abides.

"Always demanding the best of oneself, living with honor,
devoting one's talents and gifts to the benefits of others - these
are the measures of success that endure when
material things have passed away."

- Gerald Ford, Former President of the United States

Review

1. Listing of the six questions asked on my survey.

✍

2. What are your base values?
We each must decide our core values that are our truth. They include honesty, integrity, sincerity, commitment, perseverance, compassion, love, courage, trust, humility, and many more.

✍

3. Know your own truth.
We spend most of our lives accepting other's truths instead of finding our own.

Empowerment Activity

Make a list of your personal internal values. On a scale of
1 (never) to 10 (always), write the number that best
describes how you apply this value. Your truth is in
knowing your foundational values as you strive
to create your life on a higher vibration.

Present Values   Percentage No.

1. _____   _____

2. _____   _____

3. _____   _____

4. _____   _____

5. _____   _____

6. _____   _____

7. _____   _____

8. _____   _____

9. _____   _____

10. _____   _____

You'll know where you need to improve!

Affirmation

*I choose to stand in my own truth
and know my life's values.*

Being

PART III

Sitting on the fence,

looking out in all directions,

feeling safe,

but never going anywhere.

　　　　　　　　　- Carolyn Porter

15

Choices

Everything in our life involves a choice. Sooner or later a decision must be made. And if you don't make the choice yourself you can be sure someone else will make it for you.

Every life experience was created by us by making a specific choice. If I don't like my life as it is, then I need to make better choices. So often we enjoy sitting on the proverbial fence of indecision, thinking we can somehow avoid the inevitable. We're good at that, especially when the choice involves stepping into the unknown. We allow fear to keep us on that fence. We attempt to keep one foot in the old door and gingerly begin stretching our other foot into the new doorway, thinking that if we don't like what's behind the new door we can hang on to the old space and remain "safe." Of course in this situation the mind is playing tricks. It isn't possible to go in two directions at the same time, so the ego keeps you on the fence without making a choice.

Let's say you have an old car in need of major repairs. Friends have urged you to trade it in for a newer model. But this car is like family because you've babied it and polished it and cared for it for years. You're used to it. So you keep putting it off. Then one day the inevitable happens. It quits. It just wore out and now you are faced with making the choice you needed to make sooner. You have to purchase the new car.

This happens in our life so often. We put the choice off until it hits us in the face. You've known for months you should leave your job but you hesitate. One day, out of the blue, the company decides for you by letting you go, downsizing they say. Or could it be that you are being forced into a choice that you have been putting off? The same thing happens in relationships. You have known for months or maybe years that it isn't going to work, but you are afraid to leave. This happened to me. I knew on my soul level that the marriage was over for years, but for many reasons I lingered. One day, without warning, the straw that broke the camel's back happened. I couldn't overlook the choice I needed to make anymore. It was the cosmic two-by-four.

Those cosmic two-by-fours are usually our salvation, strategically placed by angels to get our full attention. Then we can once again have the opportunity to choose. After a while, if we ignore these messages, they might leave us alone to continue wandering by ourselves. I'm so thankful my angels were persistent in getting my attention. Now I continually ask for their guidance in whatever form is necessary to keep me in line!

When we make a choice there is no right or wrong. The choice will simply take us in one direction or another, and we will experience different outcomes accordingly. If we haven't learned our lessons we will be given another opportunity with another choice. This is our birthright too, freedom of will. I personally prefer being in alignment with God's will for my life and daily surrendering my will into God's will. I don't know about you but I'm glad to be free of the pain of some of my past choices. When in alignment with God you can have confidence in what you choose because God is in you and is perfection. The only time we get into trouble is when we fall into the ego trap.

The secret to wise choices is listening to your spirit. The mind is from ego and warps us with its trickery. There's a bumper sticker that says "Don't believe everything you think!" Another phrase I heard is "Your best thinking got you where you are now." So we see that our thoughts can really contrive to make amazingly unwise choices. None are wrong, just unwise. The ego sneaks in when we least expect it and gives us data that is nothing short of propaganda. Here's an example.

You have been invited to a party that you really don't want to attend but you feel obligated to go. You stall because in your heart you know you shouldn't go. You are tired and were counting on a relaxing evening to unwind. Your ego sneaks in little thoughts like "You really have a responsibility to go. After all, it's good exposure for you in your job." Then the ego continues, "You need to mingle and can relax another day. The party will do you good as you are with friends. Let your hair down and enjoy life. You deserve it."

So you ignore your spirit's guidance to stay home and relax, knowing this truth. You pull your tired body together and go to the party. You are persuaded to have a few drinks to relax more. You make your rounds with your friends and the connections you were cajoled into believing were so important. Tiredness and the effect of the alcohol overcomes you and after a while you decide to make your exit. As you drive along the highway you find your head nodding a bit. "Pull yourself together" you tell yourself since it's only a few more miles to home. Then suddenly you see a flashing light in your rear view mirror. You panic, wondering what you did to bring this happening. The officer alerts you to the fact that you didn't stop at the last stop sign and of course that's a law. During the conversation the officer suspects you've been drinking and you are asked to get out of the car and do "the test." You fail the test and the nightmare begins. All this happened because of one choice. It wasn't a wrong choice or a right choice, just a choice. The choice is bringing different results. If you had remained home and listened to what your truth was, this scenario wouldn't be happening.

So the key to making wise choices is to listen to our inner guidance. What will best serve us, others and the planet? If we choose one way will it enhance our life and further our purpose? Will it be for our highest good? To me that's the criteria of choice. How will it benefit our life and our purpose? Is it coming from a place of love or fear? When you allowed your ego to convince you to go to the party, you were coming from the fear of not making the right connections, not being socially accepted if you didn't attend or perhaps making people angry if you didn't go. You were listening to their truth and forgetting yours. You allowed them to influence your choice.

Often the path of ego seems to be the easiest way. But most often, this path is much harder than taking the "easy" route because it requires that you compromise your ethics and morals, such as taking advantage of others for your own personal gain. It's all about walking in your truth and not allowing anyone to influence your choice. Our goal must be to serve as we spread joy through loving others.

I've referred several times in this book to getting out of your box. As a society we love security, to feel comfortable and safe. We spend our lives building this so-called security as we create this boundary around us like a box. The box can only hold so much so we make choices. We fill our box with whatever we want: partner, children, family, friends, wealth, house, social activities, sports, job, beliefs, ideas, dreams, and the list could go on for miles. None of these things are "bad." In fact they are wonderful to have and they are what the universe wants to bring us. But we get comfortable enjoying these earthly manifestations and forget why we are here. We become comfortable in our box and complacent and then we are no longer free. We have placed limits around our existence by creating the boundary of a box, choosing to play it safe and be comfortable rather than move out of that comfort zone to expand and grow.

Freedom of choice is what our country is founded on. We are blessed with this freedom but we abuse it so often. Our freedom is lost to the control of others through the negative patterns we have digested. Isn't it time to remember the land of opportunity and choose what is for our highest and best, discounting the wishes of others? Isn't it time you searched your own soul for answers rather than absorbed the negativity of others? It's your mind and it's creating your life. Make choices that uphold your divinity and advance you into realms of consciousness that uplift the universe as well as your soul. Don't stay stuck in your box that is keeping you powerless. Make the choice to step out and become who you really are.

Listen to some of the words of this time-revered song on the next page. Allow the feeling to resonate with you for they share the thoughts of this writing.

My Way

"Regrets, I've had a few, but then again, too few to mention,
I did what I had to do, and saw it through without exception.
I planned each chartered course, each careful step along the by-way,
And more, much more than this, I did it my way......

For what is a man, what has he got, if not himself, then he has not,
To say the things he truly feels,
and not the words of one who kneels.
The record shows I took the blows, and did it my way."

- English words by Paul Anka
- Original French words by Giles Thiebault
- Sung and recorded by Frank Sinatra
- Music by Jacques Revaux and Claude Francois

Review

1. Everything in our life involves choice.
We create our lives by the choices we make.

❧

2. Sometimes we sit on the fence of indecision.
We sabotage ourselves by indecision because of our fear.

❧

3. If we remain indecisive we might experience the cosmic
two-by-four.
The cosmic two-by-four is to get our attention.

❧

4. Our choices are not right or wrong, just a choice.
We experience different outcomes according to our choice.

❧

5. The secret to making wise choices is to listen
to our inner guidance.
In the stillness we know our truth.

Empowerment Activity

Write indecisive situations you are in. Write the possible choices you have for each one and how it will affect your life. Then ask, "Will this choice empower me to and propel me further in my purpose, or will it keep me "stuck" in the same place?

Situation   Choices

1. *Critical relationship*   *stay*
                                             go - move on

2. *Bad child / bad relationship*   *live w/father*
                                             continue to work on him

3. *job / moved*

4. _____

Affirmation

*I choose to align myself with God's will for my life
and in doing so, I know my choices are perfect.*

Abundantly blessed,
riches beyond measure,
our storehouse overflowing
with gratitude we live a
Life Extraordinaire!

- Carolyn Porter

16
Life Extraordinaire

I don't know about you but all my life I dreamed of having an extraordinary life, one that brought me all kinds of wonderful things to enjoy. But I believed such things were for other people, important people. Then one day I woke up to the fact that I already had a life extraordinaire, and that I'm important; the same is true for you. But it all depends on how you see it.

I am a child of God, fully connected to Divine Power that reaches far beyond my human comprehension. I am part of God who created me and everything around me, making me in essence a partner with God. God is pure love as am I. God created you as well, so your essence is also love with unlimited power. You and I are part of the same love and part of God, so we are part of each other. That makes us related spiritually!

My life became an extraordinary one when I decided it

was, so that means your life is extraordinary too if that's your perception. It is an abundant life, overflowing with the good things that we deserve to have. It's an exceptional life that goes beyond the ordinary limits of a life experience. The universe is abundant and seeks to bring us every wonderful thing imaginable, but we must believe that they are ours and bring them to us.

Life extraordinaire overflows with love as it radiates outward to the world. Because we have taken the time for self-love and appreciation, we never will run out. There is always enough because we are part of God's universe where abundance is ever-present. It all starts with our focus.

Where our energy goes is where our power is. If our thoughts are centered on lack, wanting, never having enough, struggling, or any of the various forms of fear, then that's what our life will be about. I've emphasized all through this book that what we send out is what we get back. But we've been deeply programmed with these lacking thoughts for so long that we have to make a concentrated effort to change them. In Susan Jeffers book *End the Struggle and Dance with Life*, she says,

> "When we focus on abundance, our life feels abundant; when we focus on lack, our life feels lacking. It is simply a matter of focus."

So it's back to our thoughts again. What do you want your life to look like? Envision it fully with all the emotion you can muster up. Feel it, ingest it, breathe it, live it and be it. It begins with gratitude, being grateful for all you have and all you are at this present moment. It's not about how much money you have, how big your house is, how high you are on the ladder of success, or the dreams of material gain you have. It's about the value of your life, what gifts you have within that give you abundance. When you have mastered the art of gratitude you can be happy no matter how difficult your life is or how little money you have.

But you can change your life situation if you change your thoughts. You may not create millions of dollars, but the happiness within you can be overflowing. That's what gratitude creates - happiness, not money. *When you are happy you are abundant.* Everyone knows that money cannot buy happiness, but many equate abundance with monetary prosperity. Abundance can bring us great wealth, but it needs to be the by-product rather than the focus. Our intention must be to pour love out to the world as we give of ourselves from our storehouse of abundant gifts. If our intention is on gaining material possessions we have lost our focus. Brother David Steindl-Rast, author of *The Grateful Heart,* says,

"In daily life, we must see that it is not happiness that makes us grateful, but gratitude that makes us happy."

This is so very true.

Giving is part of a life extraordinaire, giving that stems from the depth of the heart rather than the base of worldly temporaries. I had heard for months about the importance of focusing on enough instead of lack. I would do it for a few days, maybe a few weeks, and then something would come into my life and disrupt my new-found thought-consciousness. Ever been there? I'd find myself thinking lack and worrying about this or that and wondering why things didn't seem to be going the way I had envisioned them. But I soon learned that once I shifted back into enough-consciousness and was aligned again with God's abundance, things would start to change. I noticed however, that it wasn't necessarily a material shift. It was in how I viewed the circumstance. And without fail in every instance, whatever I needed would appear, whether it was money, a new connection, an opportunity I needed, and so on. Sometimes the form would be different than I expected. I'd go back to being thankful for every little miracle and Voila!, life would become abundant.

I mentioned earlier how I used to love to shop. I would save a great deal but would just buy more. Now that I no longer think as I did, the quantity is greatly reduced but is always more than enough. It is all according to my perception. This came to light when I moved from my large home into a much smaller home after my divorce. My closet in the new house was much reduced in size than the big one I had to myself, and the new closet was supposed to be for two people since it is the master bedroom closet! However, after I brought the first load of clothes, (about one fourth of what I had), my new closet was almost full. Obviously I had to make a choice. I could store the extras or get rid of them. I couldn't fit them into my closet and so I decided I'd rather give them away so someone else could benefit from their use. There were no extra closets available since two of my children were still living with me. I gave away 2/3 of my clothes. And you know what? I never missed any of them! As the months went by I thought about this and I realized that I didn't need all that I thought I needed. I also realized I had changed my focus and found that I had more than enough without the closet full of clothes. Then I observed that this shift of plenty was seeping into other areas of my life and it felt good. It had been my lack consciousness that made me feel I had to have so many clothes, always needing more. You can be sure that if I felt lack in my closet I felt lack in other areas of my life.

Our minds are all cluttered with what we don't want. If that's our focus that's what shows up. To live a life extraordinaire you must shift your thoughts to out of the ordinary. I like to call it out-of-the-box thinking. Why should you be ordinary? Why shouldn't you have great abundance in your life? Try asking for it! It's really that simple. In the Bible Jesus says, " Ask and it shall be given you, seek and you shall find…" It's already there within your reach, but you must grasp it and bring it to you. If we focus on the wealth we already have, then that wealth, whatever form it is in, will expand for us. It's such a simplistic equation but we make it hard to figure out. Besides, if we already have abundance do we really need to "get" anything?

Stop and think of all you have right now. Maybe you have an old car and would like to have a newer car that was dependable and didn't rattle and shake, or maybe you want a house of your own because you are tired of apartment living, or maybe you wish for a wonderful partner to share your life. It's fine to desire these things as long as you are grateful for the bounty you already have. At least you have a car that gets you where you want to go, a roof over your head, food to eat and many friends. Think of all the greatness within you, the talents, abilities and gifts with which you've been blessed. Realize your oneness with God. You are rich my friend!

Life extraordinaire is a happy, abundant life of freedom that expands us continually into unknown out-of-the-ordinary life experiences that propel us into new, exciting adventures of growth. This life is born of love, and because it is born of love it bears humility. When there is gratitude there is humility, and no place for the ego to rule This life proclaims empowerment and brings inner joy as you've never known before. It's a life of serenity that breeds contentment. Could you ask for anything better? Not all the money, success, recognition, honor or notoriety in the world can give you this. Life extraordinaire is Spirit at work. This beautiful life frees you from the shackles of stress and brings you peace. This life is realness.

I thank God every day multiple times for the bounty in my life, even when something difficult shows up. Since I'm part of God I really don't ask for anything because in essence it's already mine, I just say "Thank you" for bringing it to me. Say it in the present as if it's already taken place. It works every time if it comes from a sincere, loving heart and your intention is truth.

"Settling for anything less than we desire or know that we deserve is how we begin to betray ourselves, moment by moment, day by day."

- Sarah Ban Breathnach, author of Something More

Review

1. We already have a life extraordinaire.
It all depends on our perception.

2. Where we place our focus is what shows up in our life.
If we focus on lack we have lack; if we focus on abundance,
we are abundant.

3. Gratitude for what you already have is where it all begins.
If we are grateful the abundance expands.

4. Think of all you have and be grateful.
You are abundant being one with God.

Empowerment Activity

Make a list of all the wonderful people and things in your life
at this moment. Be thankful to God for all the
abundance of your gifts.

_____	_____
_____	_____
_____	_____
_____	_____
_____	_____
_____	_____
_____	_____
_____	_____
_____	_____

Get out another sheet of paper and continue!

Affirmation

I choose to acknowledge my extraordinarily abundant life.

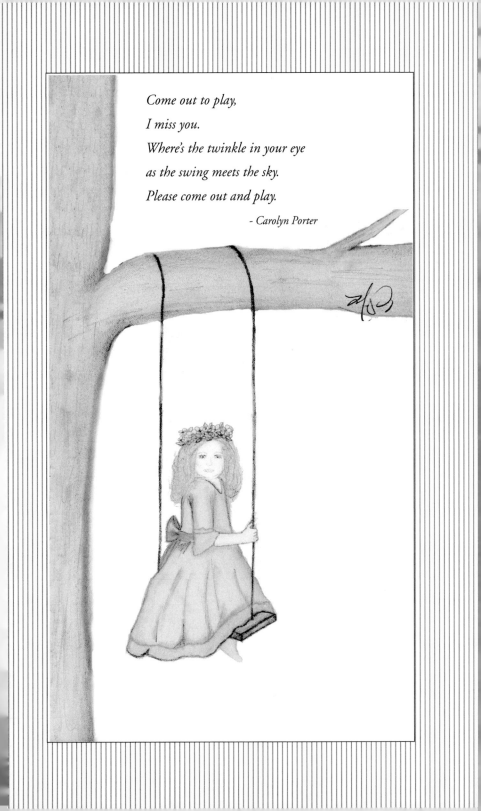

Come out to play,
I miss you.
Where's the twinkle in your eye
as the swing meets the sky.
Please come out and play.

- Carolyn Porter

17
Playtime

Do you ever go out and play? Why not? Just because we're not kids by our chronological age doesn't mean we can't play. Are you a workaholic who needs to remember those carefree childhood days? Perhaps you've heard of your inner child, that part of you that you have possibly forgotten. That inner child wants to come out to play!

Having fun is part of a balanced life. Enjoyment is part of a powerful life. Purpose work should never be anything but fun. If we consider it work then it's probably not what we should be doing. When you love what you're doing and doing what you love, it's like magic. Doesn't everyone enjoy magic?

What you consider fun might not be fun to someone else. As unique individuals we have different tastes and criteria. One person may like the movies, another bowling, another scuba diving and yet another might like to climb mountains. Whatever speaks to your heart is what's right for you. But all of us know the benefit of taking time to do something we enjoy while having fun.

What is fun? According to Webster's New World Dictionary fun is playfulness, merriment, amusement, joking, liveliness and acting foolishly. Play is motion, activity, action, rapid movement, joking and moving freely. What a wonderful way to live, in a state of merriment that allows us to joke while we move freely. I can't think of a more exciting way to live a *Life Extraordinaire,* can you? Can you imagine the panic with the drug companies if suddenly everyone began to love life and didn't need anti-depressants anymore?

Personally I love the beach. More than anything, I like to walk on the beach and at night enjoy listening to the sound of the ocean. The sea is my personal theme because it shows me the magnitude of God's power, and therefore my power. Many times as I frequented the beach I would sleep in the den area of the condo with the sliding glass doors open so I could hear the ocean sound. It touches the depth of my soul. Maybe hiking in the mountains touches the depth of your soul. I would probably enjoy hiking in the mountains as well since I enjoy walking, but I would probably select the beach as a first choice. The key is that both are individual choices that are perfect for different people. Neither is better than the other, just different, and both can reap the same benefits.

Most of us have multiple things we enjoy doing, but we often put them on the back burner because of time constraints. We're so busy doing that we omit the very thing that can help us do more in less time more efficiently - enjoy life. When's the last time you enjoyed a rip-roaring belly-shaking laugh? The kind of laugh that brings tears? Health practitioners tell us that one good laugh like that does more good than an afternoon nap. It releases endorphins and allows the blood to flow freely with a good oxygen supply. It relaxes our bodies and refreshes us. It can release myriads of tension in a few short seconds. So why not enjoy a good laugh right now!

Can you laugh at yourself when you do something silly or mess up a bit? Once we can do that we are becoming powerful beings who are okay with whoever we are at that moment. We have accepted that we don't have to do everything perfectly and we are still wonderful human beings. It also says that we love ourselves enough just the way we are.

Playtime isn't just getting away for a vacation. As nice as that is and is something we certainly should do, I'm talking about time every day to play. That could be walking or a jog, playing ball with your kids, working in your garden, taking a few minutes to tune in to God, or just relaxing in your chair for a ten minute snooze. Maybe you'd like to settle in with a great book and ignore the telephone for a few hours, or perhaps you should begin that book you want to write. A dinner out would be nice or dancing could liven your spirit, or maybe a trip to the zoo.

We get so caught up in our work that we forget to take time for fun. We have deadlines and commissions and lots and lots of self-inflicted stress from the fast-paced society in which we live. Medical reports continually tell us of the risk to our health when there's no playtime. I've been guilty of working long hours. I justified it as a necessity of starting my own business. In fact, I thought it was especially necessary I said since I was self-employed and wore all the hats in my company when it was new. It worked for a while until I began to notice a tension in my body. I just figured it was normal and ignored it. But on a particular day a friend called and suggested we do something fun. My first response was that I didn't have time. But something inside said I needed to put work aside and be refreshed. So I did.

We had a great time at a park that day. We acted like kids and I laughed more than I had for a long time. We went for a long walk and took time to breathe in nature. When the walk was finished we decided to swing on the swings. Then I got in the spirit of things and decided I'd join the kids and go down the slide. The kids looked at me like I was strange, but I did it anyway. Then I did it again. I felt so free and so alive as I became a child for a while. Can you still sing Supercalifragilisticexpialidocious or even say it for that matter? Bet you can't say it without smiling! Have you flown a kite lately or run through the sprinklers? Children know how to enjoy life because they aren't weighted down with the pressures of life. For those few hours that day I enjoyed letting go and playing. From that day forward I've allowed myself playtime much more often. And every day in some way I take time for me.

Be good to you. Does that look like a warm, relaxing candlelight bath, a facial or massage? It's important to take time to shower your physical being with acts of kindness and compassion. No one can do this for you but you, so if you don't allow a break in your busy routine you're not treasuring the gift of you.

Do something you haven't done before. That makes it an exciting adventure. Once I was at an amusement park with a couple of my children and two of my grandchildren. Most of the time I was just watching them have fun when the thought occurred that I should participate. I had never ridden the go-carts before because I usually had a baby in my arms and therefore allowed the others to do these things as I watched. But this night I had no excuse not to go since my babies had grown up. So I got in the go-cart with my youngest grandson. Once I got the hang of it I sped up and became a bit of a daredevil. My grandson was hollering "Way to go Grandma," and I was having a blast. Although it was totally out of my comfort zone before, I made the choice to do it and have some fun. It brought back many memories of my children and I riding bikes together, rollerblading, or trekking through the woods, having fun and enjoying the life of a kid.

Whatever is fun for you, do it! Open up to your inner child and invite her/him to come out and play with you. That little child can help you to see the joy in life once again, the part that you've forgotten in the hustle and bustle of living. You can then experience the wonderment of seeing through the eyes of a child.

You'll feel refreshed and alive and ready to tackle whatever you left behind as you took time to play, You might discover a rosy glow in your cheeks!

Stage set:

School is about to begin for the year as Tigger and Winnie the Pooh are discussing all the upcoming work with Christopher Robin.

"All these ABCs and 1-2-3s are fine, but what about fun? What good is a place if you can't even bounce?" said Tigger. Christopher Robin replied, "My school has a playground and we get to go outside and play nearly every day. We have a real playground with slides and swings and everything." So Tigger says, "I knew Tiggers loved school!"

Note: Taking time for fun makes any job more tolerable and maybe even enjoyable.

Review

1. Do you ever go out and play?
We need to bring back the fun of childhood.

☙

2. What is fun?
Fun is merriment, activity, motion, feeling free.

☙

3. Playtime is not just vacation.
*Take breaks every day for relaxation. Act like a kid
and play with your inner child.*

Empowerment Activity

What do you enjoy doing? Don't think; just write.

_____   _____

_____   _____

_____   _____

_____   _____

_____   _____

_____   _____

_____   _____

_____   _____

DO THEM!

Affirmation

*I choose to enjoy life more by bringing
out my inner child to play.*

Dream your dream,
breathe in imagination;
look beyond the impossible
for there is the possible.

- Carolyn Porter

18

See the Horizon

All dreams are possible if you change your limited perception of what is possible. Most people don't believe that. They may speak it from their mouths but it doesn't register in their hearts and souls. And yet there isn't anything you cannot do if you truly want to do it.

What is on your horizon? What would you like your life to look like? What are your dreams? What would you really like to do that would benefit humanity? In what way would you like to make a difference in our world?

Ask yourself this question: If money was no issue because I had more money than I could ever spend in this lifetime and I could do anything I wanted to do, what would it be? Look deep into your soul and let the answer flow effortlessly forth. Just imagine that you never had to work again but could do anything, absolutely anything, you wanted to do. What would that look like for you? If it isn't exactly what you are presently doing then you need to grab your paintbrush and start a new picture.

In the July, 2003 issue of Oprah magazine, Oprah says this

"I know for sure that what we dwell on is who we become - as a woman thinketh, so is she. If we absorb hour upon hour of images and messages that don't reflect our magnificence, it's no wonder we walk around feeling drained of our life force. Become the change you want to see - those are words I live by. I don't know how many years I'll be blessed with the privilege of reaching millions each day, but my prayer is that I'll use my energy never to belittle but to uplift. Never to devastate but to rebuild. Never to misguide but to light the way so that all of us can stand on higher ground."

This entire book has been for you to see that you can create the life you've always dreamed about. The first step is knowing what you want to create. Begin at your core and know on what you are building your life. Just as an artist cannot paint without the basic colors, you cannot create a life design without knowing your foundational values. Is your foundation seated on principles that elevate your soul onto a higher level?

At the time I decided to become a public speaker I saw that I would speak to many people but I couldn't feel it. In fact, I doubted my capabilities but I knew in my heart that it was part of my purpose. As I took small steps and began to experience small audiences, I began to *feel* what it was like to be a speaker. I had to break through the fear barrier to experience the love of what I am now doing. The more I opened my heart to my audiences and what I was sharing, the more realistic it became because I *felt* the experience. I was keeping my vision alive.

The core of becoming is focusing on the vision of your life. We've talked endlessly about the power of your thoughts and how

they create your life. Whatever you dwell on is what you create. I
saw what I felt God wanted me to do and I continually focused on
it. I would envision it with feeling, seeing myself in various speaking
arrangements and imagining what it would feel like. I made a collage
of pictures that I imagined would occur and kept it where I could
see it every day. I never stopped seeing it or painting it into the
design of my life, and it happened. I also created affirmations that
said exactly what I wanted in the present, as if it had already
happened, and I repeated them multiple times each day. When
preparing for my first seminar I affirmed "I am speaking with ease
and the audience is attentively listening," and it happened!

At first I would be in awe that it happened as I had drawn the
picture. But the more it happened the more exciting it became
until I would actually anticipate the next step, knowing beforehand
what it would be. Of course I didn't know the details of how it
would happen, but it always came about as I had drawn it.

It was then that I realized my power - that what I wanted was
right there if I believed it was there. But it went further than just
me. I realized that everyone can create exactly what they want just
as I am doing. The only thing that can ever get in your way is
yourself. So, is it about time for you to get out of your way and use
your power to manifest your dreams? Be a player in your life, not
just on the sideline!

I used to read my kids a story called *The Little Engine That
Could*. They all loved the story and we read it over and over. This
little engine had to take over for the big engine and pull the rest of
the train up the mountain. No one believed he could do it; they all
said he was too small and didn't have enough strength. But the
little engine determined he could and continued to try. He struggled
and summoned every ounce of his strength. He went through all
kinds of difficulties but he never gave up because he knew he could
make it. And he did make it with everyone cheering! An age-old

fairytale that we women always loved, Cinderella, who was abused and made to feel inferior by her "family," had a heart that was of love. She dreamed of something different and her dream came true because she never lost sight of it. In both of these stories we see real truths for us. Maybe we should pull those children's books from our basement storage and re-read these simple truths.

Our ego is the culprit for the detour signs on the road to claiming our power. Throughout the previous pages I've examined many phases of our own self-abuse so that we could move out of the dungeon and see the light. Our brilliance is waiting to shine forth but we must let go of all that doesn't enhance our beauty. In her book *One Day My Soul Just Opened Up*, Iyanla Vanzant reviews much of what I've shared when she wrote

> "Ego, is that part of us that continues to worry, lives in doubt, is afraid, judges other people, is afraid to trust, needs proof, believes only when it is convenient, fails to follow up, refuses to practice what it preaches, needs to be rescued, wants to be a victim, beats upon 'self,' needs to be right all of the time and continues to hold onto whatever does not work."

Holding the vision and continually placing it in our view is integral in creating our dreams, but there's another aspect that cannot be forgotten - action. Without action the vision is only a daydream. Daydreams can revitalize our spirit, and adding a goal to it makes it even more real, but without the forward movement it won't become reality. We often need reinforcement techniques to help us move ahead.

Robert Byrne states: "There are two kinds of people, those who finish what they start and so on." Let's say a person has a dream to become a musician or to make a living as an artist. Perhaps he wants to become president of a company, write a book or open a restaurant. He thinks about his dream often and talks about it with his friends. He thinks about it while sleeping and is even spurred on by self-help/motivational books. He creates goals.

But it never happens. His 20's turn into 30's and soon become his 40's. Before you know it he's reached the 50's and his dream is gone. He has allowed others to figure out his life for him and he lets go of his dream. Then he wonders what happened. Nine times out of ten it's been said that dreamers fail not because they didn't create goals but because they didn't turn the goals into action steps. Many people listen to ego thoughts and get in their own way. One technique that can help create accountability is something that costs nothing and is simple to execute, yet can yield the desired achievement of your dream.

It has been said by many successful people that spending 1000 hours on something can give you the desired goal. Create a chart with a grid of 1000 boxes. Place it where you can easily see it throughout your day. Every time you spend an hour doing something specifically useful in the process of achieving your goal, blacken a box. By the time you have completed marking out the 1000 boxes you will probably have achieved your goal. As you go through this process you will see abundance in many forms flow to you. If you want to achieve your dream, you must spend the time it requires to get there. *Don't leave this planet with your dream still inside of you.*

We came into this lifetime to heal and be healed. No matter what we decide to do in our life, it is part of our healing. The healing ensues through the choices we make and the lessons of growth we experience. The only way we can create a future from the present moment is to let go of the past. Once we let go we open up the space for the miracles. As we allow the miracle of healing in us, we empower others to do the same. *As looking in a mirror, what empowers others also empowers you.*

And so it seems our lives are *being* at this moment. You are becoming whatever you have thought you should be. Every experience you materialize is of your mind. How do you see yourself? Do you see yourself as the valuable priceless jewel you are? A gift to this world? A woman that will leave her mark for the world to see? Do you really *know* this?

If you still doubt your own worthiness even a tiny bit, perhaps the following will help to convince you that you can choose to be bigger than you see yourself now.

Marilyn Monroe once failed to get a modeling job.

Michael Jordon was cut from his high school basketball team.

Walter Cronkite failed a radio announcer's test.

Henry Ford never went past sixth grade in school.

Oprah Winfrey had great difficulty when she was a news reporter in Baltimore. She was pressured to remain detached from the stories she covered while her whole being wanted to empathize. She was told she was being demoted from a reporter to a talk show host. She allowed this perceived failure by many to become her greatest opportunity.

All of these examples give us more validation that we have genius within. Each of these giants experienced difficulty but kept their vision alive and moved forward regardless. Know your greatness!

Marianne Williamson tells the story about a woman she knows who wears a thin gold chain around her waist, under her clothes, with a charm bearing the inscription *Priceless*. It drives men crazy apparently. She says the men love to be reminded of what they already know but are in a world that constantly denies it. She says she wears the chain in such a way that the charm falls perfectly across a certain female chakra to remind her constantly of her inestimable value.

What a great idea! Something that reminds us constantly of our worthiness that is beyond measure. Perhaps we should all own such a chain and charm. We need to be reminded every day that we cannot be put down any longer. We are strong and noble and are blessed. We do not bow to anyone for we are goddesses.

You were born with wings to fly. You are here to become as you remember who you are. If we take away the old beliefs, the resistance, the attachments, the fear, the questions, the busyness, the drifting, the powerlessness, the indecision, the deceptiveness, the lack and the struggle, what is left? Your naked divinity. You stand there completely vulnerable as you stretch your arms out to the universe. You are a goddess, full of the brightest light and the richest, deepest love imaginable because you reflect God's love and light. This is who you are - God's light-beam expressing to the world. Imagine, millions of light-beams splintering from Divine Light to the far corners of the earth as we illumine the world with our magical love.

Look through the eyes of God at what is righteous and uplifting as you look beyond to what will honor your spirit. Do not look through someone else's eyes for your dream. As another's glasses do not help you see clearly, neither do their eyes. Seek your heart's desire within the recesses of your higher self. Know the preciousness of life as it abounds before *your* eyes, and include yourself in that preciousness. Dream the impossible dream for there is no impossible dream. You can create whatever you desire as you look to the horizon of your life. Reach out, expand, become, and allow yourself to rise above "self" as you lift your hand to the hand of God. What is your dream? Begin now as you place it in your life's horizon.

Become your dream!

> *"All our dreams can come true if we have the*
> *courage to pursue them."*

> *- Walt Disney, Cartoon Artist and Producer*

1. All dreams are possible if we believe they are.
Most people know this in their head but not in their heart.

෴

2. We must envision what we want for our life.
The vision must be kept alive and we must feel it.

෴

3. Our ego is a master at detour signs.
Don't allow your ego to disrupt your path of healing.

෴

4. Use the technique of working 1000 hours toward
achieving your goal.
*This process has helped many to achieve their goal
because it requires action steps.*

෴

5. Every one of you are priceless!
*We need to see ourselves through the eyes of God -
divine beings expressing light.*

Empowerment Activity

Create your future!

1. Make a collage of pictures that show what you want your life to look like. Place it where you can look at it every day.

2. Visualize as many goals for your life as you wish, one at a time. Put feelings into this vision and be sure to include as many of the senses as possible:

Sight

Sound

Smell

Taste

Touch

Intuition

Affirmation

I choose to know that I can do anything
I desire, since I am a child of God.

Radiating out from the innerspace
of your heart,
there is only love.
God's love and you are one.

- Carolyn Porter

19

Your Divine Essence

For many pages I've been sharing how great you are. You are beautifully and wonderfully made from a magnificent design. You are a tower of strength with unlimited possibilities that can touch the hearts of mankind. In the words of Reverend Charlotte Beilgard,

"Like a magnificent rose you are in the garden of life,
you deserve happiness without any strife.
You can relax and re-learn how to play,
be the somebody that loves you everyday.
Take time to nurture yourself, you're worth the cost;
re-claim your authentic power that seems so lost.
Feel your fear but trust your faith to see you through,
change your mind, accept and celebrate being the
authentic You!"

That's what you are - a magnificent rose in the garden of

life, waiting to open into the fullness of your beauty. You are of God, which is pure love. There is nothing more beautiful than love shining from your soul. You have unlimited power that can make you the master of your life.

It's a sad era as we realize how many women are afraid to shine their light. It's sad that so many women hide behind their perceived inferiority when they are part of the kingdom of God. Think about that for a minute. You are part of God's kingdom, one of his magnificent creations, capable of unlimited potential, a spiritual being who is one with the Creator of the universe, all powerful and only born of love. How could you be inferior? You are a superior being, and the deepest fear you feel is your unlimited power. It isn't the fear of failing in this life that frightens most people, but it's the fear that they might be seen, that they really are powerful and really can do mighty works. It means they must step up to the plate if they claim their power for the world to see. Grabbing your birthright and becoming what your spirit wants is exactly what your ego fights against. Your ego doesn't want you to shine, for if you shine with the light of God through you the ego must retreat into the darkness.

Our ancestors knew only the teachings of their forefathers. They taught us to be afraid. They taught us to remain in our "place" according to what they knew. We have felt lesser, unworthy, defective, undeserving, lacking, restricted and unloved for many years. We believed it and made it our life experience. But isn't it incredible that all this time we only had to remember who we are and what we are here to do.

Do you see the power within you? You were born with it and you've always owned it. You came from it and can claim it at any time. Your possibilities are endless. Nothing will ever touch the depth of your soul more than knowing that because you sent love out to people, you have helped them make positive changes in their life. Nothing will ever humble your spirit more than the knowing that through your love someone else became empowered. Nothing will ever bring joy overflowing from your heart than when someone comes to you and says "Thank you for taking the time to help me on my path. Because of your love I have been able to transform my life." Tears will fill your eyes as you leave your comfortable box and step into the unknown, knowing you are making a difference in this world. You are truly empowered!

Read carefully what Marianne Williamson has said so beautifully in *A Woman's Worth*:

> "Our deepest fear is not that we are inadequate.
> Our deepest fear is that we are powerful beyond measure.
> It is our light, not our darkness that frightens us.
> We ask ourselves, who am I to be brilliant, gorgeous, talented and fabulous?
> Actually, who are you not to be? You are a child of God.
> Your playing small does not serve the world.
> There is nothing enlightened about shrinking so that other people won't feel insecure around you.
> We are all meant to shine, as children do.
> We are born to manifest the glory of God that is within us.
> It's not just within some of us; it's in everyone.
> And as we let our own light shine, we unconsciously give other people permission to do the same.
> As we are liberated from our own fear, our presence automatically liberates others."

> "When a woman conceives her true self, a miracle occurs and life around her begins again."

We have a responsibility to shine all over the world. You came here to complete a mission. Your spirit is waiting for you to move from selfishness to selflessness. It isn't easy to move along your path when the world fights you and tries to block you. It isn't easy when the shadows of darkness flaunt trinkets of temporary pleasure to entice you away from your path. It isn't easy to stand in your light, shining alone at times, as others seem to move away from you. But who will carry the torch? Who but you can stand in your light and make the choice to empower others so you too can be empowered?

There is a big shift occurring on our planet. People by the droves are seeking spiritual awakening. People are searching for the lightworkers who can light the way for them. People want more depth in themselves, in their relationships, and in their life. Their soul reaches out for guidance and support, and we are the ones they reach.

Each of us has our own uniqueness. Each of us is an individual who, although connected spiritually to the collective energy force of the universe, is unique in her own right. We strive for identity in this world. We want to belong to something and/or someone. Yet we are unique individuals who cannot be as other beings. We are with God, of God and from God, yet each of us has a unique story to live. We must be ourselves and cannot be like another. This means we cannot belong, we simply are.

I recently became aware of this insight in a practical application in one of my life experiences. I was visiting some of my family. Although family togetherness can sometimes show lack of togetherness, I decided before going that I would have no expectations of the visit and would only shower everyone with love. I was not going with the intent of gaining anything, but only to give. The entire experience was delightful. I viewed the trip differently. Although some family members were more loving than others, I remained detached from their issues and thoroughly enjoyed every minute.

But as I sat at the table during one meal, I felt very absent. I heard the conversation and entered in at times, but thoughts continually raced through my mind. I thought, "I don't fit here.

I'm not like any of these people. How could these individuals be my family? Where do I belong?" I felt as if I was in an altered state. Then my thoughts went to my children. They are all grown with their own lives. I remembered how I used to think they'd be mine forever; I had seen no end to diapers, skinned knees, sports games and proms for so many years as a mother of five children. The thoughts were a bit unsettling as I continued through the day. Where exactly did I fit? I was alone. I had stood for my truth which most did not share.

Later that day, as I looked out the window of the plane that was taking me back home, and the thoughts were again with me, I suddenly understood. I am unique. I am me, Carolyn. I am like no one else, I cannot be like anyone else, and I wouldn't want to be like anyone else. I realized that I am not meant to "fit" but to stand out in my truth as me, a spiritual being. I realized my thoughts had been from past programming that wanted me to conform to the mold of others. I looked out at the peacefulness and serenity in the beautiful blue sky that surrounded the plane and reached to the heavens. I felt as if I was basking in divine love with so much magnificence enveloping me. Imagine the genius that could actually create an airplane that would remain in the air and transport me so quickly to my destination. Imagine the genius that imagined a way to schedule planes so they take off and land continually. Imagine the genius that could actually fly this craft safely. I was struck with the awesomeness of God and the fact that we are part of this power. Each of us is a genius if we allow this knowingness.

So I realized that day that I was not meant to "fit." As a woman of realness I cannot "fit" anywhere except within me. Although family ties are wonderful in the physical dimension, they are not to bind us, but to free us. There is no judgment in the relationships so there can be no "fit." People often expect the earthly ties to give them their identity and bind them together simply because it's more comfortable that way. Instead, we should be helping our family members as well as all other beings to expand past these ties and become the people they are meant to be, standing in their own truth. Then the family ties are from love and recognize each individual's uniqueness.

I am a lightworker who chose to come here and shine my light throughout the world. I am in alignment with God's will and therefore "fit" only with God. God directs my path as I listen and follow. I didn't always follow so willingly because I allowed my ego to rule. Each of you can be a lightworker if you choose to be. We can be likened to the imperial lighthouse that lights the way in the darkness so the ships are able to find their way. We are helping mankind to find its way.

Look at yourself as a divine farmer. You carry a bag of many seeds from the light. Your responsibility is to plant those seeds where you are guided. Then you must cultivate the ground, mix in the nutrients, and pray for the sun and rain to immerse the earth. You wait, with patience, always holding the faith for the abundant field of harvest that is coming. It doesn't happen overnight. Sometimes drought or wind or pestilence can wear the farmer down. Sometimes the seedlings wither and die. Sometimes the farmer is so tired from all the long hours and labor that his heart grows weary. But then, one day as he looks out over the fields, he sees the magnificent harvest of his efforts. His loving heart was in every step of the way and now he reaps what he sowed.

And so my friend, you are a farmer of God with your own bag of seeds. Have you begun to plant them yet? Are you ready to do the work? God's work is not for the faint in heart. Can you hold the faith when challenges line your path? Are you ready to stand firm in your own truth instead of bowing to the perceptions of others?

This is your calling, to stand firm in your truth only. You must follow your inner guidance and listen with your heart. Your heart is the thermostat by which you can measure your response with the world. The warmer it is the more open you are. The more open you are the more truth flows from you. What does your heart look like? Do you see compassion, gratitude, appreciation, and kindness oozing out of you? Do you feel love swell up inside towards all beings? Or do you save that for a few "special" people? Perhaps you see shadows of darkness lurking in the corners and big walls blocking the light. Are there old rotting patterns that feel heavy in your heart? Do you realize that whatever is on the inside of you is what everyone on the outside sees?

Take a moment to understand the feeling of love in your heart. It's yours and yours alone. The color pink reflects love. Imagine your heart filled with soft pink love. See beautiful golden lightbeams radiating out from your heart that's filled and overflowing with pink love. Feel the warmth of that light pulsating. Now feel your heart expand as the heat from the pink love bubbles up inside. Your heart is swelling and it feels as if it will jump out of your chest. Feel the depth of that love as it swirls throughout your body, spreading warmth from head to toe, overtaking your very breath as you reel from its vastness. Take it all in. Feel every dimension of that love, as if God's arms, joined with a whole host of angels' wings are wrapped around you, for they are. Feel the awesomeness of being one with God as you are encompassed by divine love. You are that love. You came from that love, it lives within you, you are one with it and it is always present. There are really no human words that can rightfully express the depth and breath of this love because it surpasses any known emotional expression on this planet. Once you have felt this love, you will understand the inadequacy of human words in the expression of the spiritual kingdom.

As you feel the love in you, visualize it radiating outward from you, beams of light coming out of your body and shooting energy in every direction. Visualize the beams projecting to family members, friends, acquaintances, co-workers, to people all over the world like missiles finding their target. Congratulations! You are the light. Hold on to this for this is your divine essence.

Your search is to find this love and become it. To become love is to heal your soul. As you heal your soul, you allow the planet to do the same. You are here to heal through the life lessons you chose to experience that enable you to remember your beingness. As a holy being you know your divine essence is love. This is your realness.

May today there be peace within...

May you trust your highest power that you are exactly where you are meant to be...

May you not forget the infinite possibilities that are born of faith...

May you use those gifts that you have received, and pass on the love that has been given to you...

May you be content knowing you are a child of God...

Let this presence settle into your bones, and allow your soul the freedom to sing and dance...

It is there for each and every one of you...

- St. Theresa Prayer

Review

1. Each of us is a beautiful rose in the garden of life.
Most women suffer from defectiveness.

2. Your power is within you already.
You were born with it and have always owned it.

3. It is meant for you to stand in your own light.
People want to "fit" with something or someone.

4. Knowing divine love is your soul's purpose.
You are love and are here to shine your light.

Empowerment Activity

Write down ways you have demonstrated your divine power.

1. _____

2. _____

3. _____

4. _____

5. _____

Now look at each of the above and observe how it made you feel as you felt your power.

Use these observations to implement into all areas of your life.

Affirmation

I choose to become love for it is my divine essence.

To have the love that we do want
'tis that which we must be,
the mirror can only reflect
and share what it can see.

- Carolyn Porter

20

Attracting Love

Love is all there is. Be the love you want - that's how you attract it. We have been on a journey throughout this book to enlighten you with the knowingness of love, how you are love, and to bring it into your life. It is simple: Be Love.

There is no other way to experience real love. There are no side roads or shortcuts. There are no alternative routes. You cannot buy it, fake it, manifest for it or create it in any way until you are that love. You cannot know it until it knows you. The law of attraction has always been and will always be that "like attracts like." Unless you are the love you want you will never find it!

We've spoken of the outpouring of love through these expressions: compassion, gratitude, appreciation, kindness, generosity, encouragement, willingness, acceptance, allowing, empowerment, strength, patience, caring and surrender. Being love and giving love is how we receive it.

I've heard over the years that there are different kinds of love. I don't agree with that statement. Love is love, all part of the universal love of God. How could you ever measure different levels of love? Do you think God has a storehouse of different kinds of love with labels from which we pick the one that works for a particular relationship?. That's kind of absurd isn't it? I believe there is only love, but we do have different responses according to the relationship we are experiencing.

Consider the simple act of breathing. It's essential to stay alive. It's always there for us and it's free for the taking. We can have it anytime we want. There aren't different kinds of air. It's simply air. However, we can respond to it differently. If we are jogging we might use more air at a quicker rate. If we're meditating we might take slow, deep breaths to relax us. If we've just missed being in an accident we might be experiencing short, shallow breaths from the adrenal rush. As we swim below the surface of the water we actually stop breathing for a few moments. Our response to the air is different in various circumstances, but it doesn't alter the air. The air is always the same and is always present as air.

Loving ourselves and sharing that love with the world is what our life is about. We never know when a spoken word or kind gesture will change someone's life. Let me share two stories with you.

Here's a story told by a boy named Dave:

"One day, as a freshman in high school, I saw a kid from my class walking home from school. His name was Kyle. His arms were full of books and I wondered why anyone would take all his books home on a Friday. I shrugged my shoulders and turned toward home because I had a big weekend planned.

A few minutes later I saw a bunch of kids running toward Kyle. They knocked him down so that all his books went scattering

everywhere as his glasses went flying. My heart went out to him so I ran over to help him. A tear was rolling down his face as I handed him his glasses and helped him gather his books. I told him the other guys were real jerks and he said 'Thanks' as he smiled big.

I walked with him to his house and learned he had gone to private school before so hadn't gotten too well acquainted in this area. We began to 'hang out' and I liked him. We became friends for the next four years of high school.

Soon it was time for graduation. Kyle was going to be a doctor and was headed to Georgetown while I was going for business on a football scholarship at Duke. I teased him about being a nerd because he was to be the class valedictorian. I was just glad it wasn't me having to get up there in front of all those people.

When it was time for Kyle to give his speech, he cleared his throat and looked out over the class. Then he began. 'Graduation is a time to thank those who helped you make it through those tough years. Your parents, your teachers, your siblings, maybe a coach…but mostly your friends. I am here to tell all of you that being a friend to someone is the best gift you can give them. I am going to tell you a story.'

I looked at my friend in disbelief as he recounted the story of the first day we met. He had planned to kill himself over the weekend. He talked of how he had cleaned out his locker so his Mom wouldn't have to do it later so was carrying his stuff home when the other kids attacked him. He looked at me hard and smiled. He went on…'Thankfully I was saved. My friend saved me from doing the unspeakable.'

The crowd gasped as this now popular young man told about his weakest moment. His Mom and Dad were looking at me and smiling the same kind of smile as he was. It wasn't until this moment that I realized the depth of my one act of kindness.

Now here's a story from one of my own life experiences:

Some years back, as I was actively running one of our health stores, a customer came in and shared about a friend of his. He told me the friend was depressed and quite sick and knowing my willingness to help him in the past, asked if I would call this man and talk to him. Apparently he was too sick to drive and lived a considerable distance away. I said I would gladly call and obtained the man's phone number.

That night I called the man. He was depressed and full of anger and was very sick. I gave him some suggestions of places to go for help as well as some guidelines for supplements that he could choose. I listened throughout the hour and a half conversation as he dropped little comments about not wanting to go on. It was then I suggested he see a counselor or psychologist, but he refused saying he was broke and jobless and didn't trust just anybody. So I asked God to give me the words because I knew this was out of my expertise.

I told him I would be happy to talk again, but that he should call me. He called me every night for a week and we talked. I so wanted to help him and let him know he could make it if he really wanted to - that there was hope. Then he began missing some nights and after a couple weeks it became a weekly conversation. He was still on this planet so I was glad for that, but I wasn't sure if I was helping very much. The calls got further apart and after about six months the calls abruptly stopped. I was concerned but knew it was out of my hands. His friend who originally asked me to call him came in the store a few months later and informed me that he had gone to live with his sister in another state who was helping him continue toward regaining his health.

Almost a year and a half later as I was helping a customer in my store one day, a man came in and patiently waited until I was finished with the customer. After finishing with the customer I

went over to him and asked if I could help him. He replied as he
gave me his name, "Do you remember me? I'm the guy you talked
to for hours about a year and a half ago." Instantly the whole
picture came pouring into my mind. He continued by saying:
"Because of you I am here today. I had to come by and meet you
and say thank you." Even as I write this the goose bumps are
traveling up and down my body as I remember that moment
when I realized what had occurred. He said he was working
now, had a girlfriend and felt good about life. Wow!

I will never forget that moment as long as I live. I thought
about what might have happened had I not taken the time to talk
with that man. It wasn't part of my normal routine of owning a
health store even though we were always about helping people.
But I'm so glad I felt led to talk with him. We never know what
one small gesture can do to change a person's life or how at any
given moment we can become an earth angel for someone's needs.
I heard this quote once although I don't know its origin: "Friends
are angels who lift us to our feet when our wings have trouble
remembering how to fly." This is the realness of love.

No matter what relationships we attract into our lives, they
will be reflections of who we are on the inside. If we are needy we
will attract a needy person. This relationship will depend on the
ego's manipulation to supply the emptiness within the individuals.
Of course that emptiness will never be filled because another person
cannot fill us. If you have a pattern of attracting addictive partners,
you'll continue doing this until you get the lesson and break the
chain.

Attracting a partner that we really don't want happens so many
times when a person leaves one relationship and immediately jumps
into another. Without the void time there hasn't been healing and
the same core issues will be there with a different face and the same
experience will be repeated until the lesson is learned. But if there's

healing time that allows recognizing and releasing the old patterns as new beliefs replace them, then a truly desirable person is drawn to them.

So you've been working on yourself and you say you feel love for yourself. You believe it's time to bring a partner into your life. Ask yourself this question: "Do I love myself enough to marry me?" If you can say "yes" than you're ready, but if it's "no" then you'd better stop right there or you'll attract someone other than you desire. Maybe you never thought about marrying yourself. If you don't want you, why do you think anyone else would?

A relationship is not about fixing someone. How many times have you heard someone say as they're contemplating a committed relationship, "I don't like this about him but I'll work on him and change him." And who got the last laugh with that one? We cannot change another person. A relationship based on Spirit is for the purpose of showing the power of God.

So we must come from a spiritual base in building our relationships. If more people would begin with Spirit and then bring in the physical realm, more relationships would be nurturing and healing. As they are, many relationships begin with the physical chemistry and don't often get past that connection. History shows that the physical chemistry can wear off rather quickly. There's research to indicate that 80% of people in broken relationships knew before the vows were exchanged that this union wasn't right, but they did it anyhow. Good grief! What are people thinking?

How do you attract the "right" partner for you? The first step is to be the love you want; it won't work any other way. Then you state clearly to the universe exactly what you want in your partner. A friend of mine shared an exercise and suggested I do this. He said to write down on paper everything I wanted in my partner. Then he told me to call him back when I was finished. When I called he had me read them out loud without him making any comments.

Then...he asked me if there were any of these qualities that I didn't do. I replied that there were four out of the nineteen that I didn't do well. So he simply said, "Go work on those four things about yourself until they are right and then the partner will appear." I certainly wasn't expecting that, but it sure brought to light the entire principle of like attracts like. *Whatever you want in your partner you must be it first.* The beauty of it is that as you seek the person of your dreams you become the dream person. That's pretty incredible isn't it?

I've been guided to share the first ten (out of my 19) qualities I want in my ideal partner. Yours may be totally different and that's okay, but maybe this will help you understand the process. These are in the order of importance to me at this writing.

1. Honesty - with himself and with others
2. Deeply spiritual
3. A loving heart
4. Following his purpose - has his own mission
5. My best friend
6. Passionate about life - energetic
7. Enjoys the simple things, especially nature
8. Creative
9. Accepts me as I am
10. Is into health and fitness

The other qualities I listed are also important, but these are the top ten. The universe wants to bring you what you want so lay it out with specifics. Then let it go. I'm referring to divine timing, patience, allowing - all those things we don't want to acknowledge. Letting it go means allowing for God's timing, not ours.

Another way to attract the "perfect" partner is through living your purpose. I read a story about a woman who was searching for her partner but he was eluding her. She had decided to train for a ten-kilometer race on a steep mountain even though she wasn't sure she could do it. This had been a dream of hers so she committed to the process. She won her age category and was standing on the podium totally exhilarated when another runner noticed her and how she glowed. He knew he had to meet her and a very happy marriage followed. She pushed her limits and followed her dream and her "perfect" partner showed up.

Martha Beck wrote the following article in an Oprah magazine

> "To find a mate, don't become someone you're not. Dare to be more yourself. Push yourself beyond what you think are your limits, and you may discover that the love you want is running right beside you, through the territory you were born to inhabit."

Aren't we fantastic at showing up for a partner all dolled up in our best duds? We could easily be actresses for the way we scheme and play charades. We aim to please and we hide things about ourselves because we're making a good impression. We've all done it and maybe you're still doing it. What's going to happen when the paint wears off and the bare metal is exposed? Be yourself, through and through, the real you. I remember hearing a friend say that we must market (sell) ourselves to our partner continuously all through the relationship. What a pressure! How can we be ourselves if we're always trying to sell someone on our best qualities? Would that be trying to convince because fear rules? What might the other person think if they knew the real you? When would the wounds be made visible and the healing begin? Be your authentic self!

Partners must share the enthusiasm for each other's purpose in life. Since your purpose becomes your life and is your passion for life, how can you have an incredible relationship if you don't share in each other's dreams? But at the same time you cannot forget your own purpose by getting lost in the dreams of your partner. This has been the pattern of so many committed relationships; it must be broken. To me it's a prerequisite that each partner share in the others purpose in order to have an intimate, loving relationship with God and for healing.

Once you know who you are and are empowered in your own truth, then your partner can appear. You deserve the best and should never accept anything less than the best. If you don't know your worth, you will not realize it by having the approval of others. As a woman of realness you won't need this person's approval of you, just acceptance. And that's what unconditional love is - total acceptance without judgment. It allows the individual to be an individual, unique in their own right, and perfect being one with God. Don't ever sell your soul to anyone. Remember who you are, a divine being of divine love, and worthy of every good and perfect gift. Your real identity is founded in Spirit while everything else is a fleeting moment in time.

Let me share an incredible story that was related in *I Had It All the Time* by Alan Cohen. This story is the epitome of unconditional love that is truly birthed from the depths of a heart in alignment with divine love.

Alan was staying in the home of a friend during a lecture tour. The host and his wife were obviously very much in love and had been together over 50 years. One might wonder what their secret is. The next morning the host joined Alan for a few moments to talk before the busy day began. He had brought a photo with him and showed it to Alan. The photo was of a bestselling author and was recognized immediately. The host tells his story.

"Many years ago I met this author and was irresistibly drawn to her. I tried to forget her and hide the thoughts from my wife, but she knew and I could no longer keep the secret. I told her I wanted to spend time with this author. His wife was quiet for a moment then said, 'I can't give you everything. If this is what you want, then go do it. There is not enough love in the world.

I can't and won't stop you. I want you to be happy.' So I went, had this affair, then realized it wasn't to continue anymore. I came home and fell into my wife's arms, weeping. She was still there, loving me as she always had."

Is there a better example of unconditional love? I can't imagine what it could be. I'm not saying we should allow our partners to have affairs and then come back as if nothing ever happened, but this exemplifies what unconditional love can do in a relationship. It means loving this person enough to let him go if need be, because you want nothing but happiness for him. It is selfless love, all born of divine love. In the following poem, Kahlil Gibran affirms this love:

Love gives naught but itself and takes naught but from itself.
Love possesses not nor would it be possessed;
For love is sufficient unto love…
Love has no other desire but to fulfill itself…
To wake at dawn with a winged heart and give thanks
for another day of loving…
And then to sleep with a prayer for the beloved in your heart
and a song of praise upon your lips.

This is the love that originates from the heart of God. It is not based on expectations, manipulation, judgment, approval, codependency or anything else from ego's intentions. It is love that stands in spirit and radiates from the heart to every thought, word, action and response. It is not based on anything material, but only on the power of God. *This love is the essence of a woman of realness.* It is a love you have for yourself, that completes your beingness— whether or not you have a mate, whether or not you have children, whether or not you are wealthy, whether or not you have anything you think you need to be happy. With this love you have touched a higher spiritual vibration that shows your realness and you know you are a woman of worth. You are no longer lonely, for you have yourself.

Physical Attraction

The physical attraction between two people is obvious when they meet. Whether it becomes a personal or business relationship, there must be a chemistry that attracts. The chemistry has a different meaning depending on the nature of the relationship.

I think it's sad that today's society emphasizes physical intimacy. It seems that this kind of relationship is based on how great it makes you feel sexually, how often you can perform, how many different experiences you can have, how well you can perform, or with how many partners you can "score." Physical intimacy is a wonderful part of a relationship, but if the basis of a relationship is on performance and temporary gratification instead of the depth of spiritual connection, it will soon lose its sexual appeal. It isn't possible to be real if you must always live up to certain expectations.

It is possible to be totally satisfied spiritually even though physical needs are not being met. Physical completion is passing and quickly fades away and is never completely satisfied, like an insatiable thirst. On the other hand, spiritual completion fills you up with a feeling of total satisfaction. If you combine the two you have the epitome of unification, a holy encounter with God, with total sexual and spiritual completion.

Physical union is sacred, but many have no thoughts for the holiness of their encounter; it is strictly for physical pleasure. Our society has cheapened a holy encounter by reducing it to lust. Our sexuality is actually our creativity. Sexual energy does not just mean physical intimacy; it is also our creativity center for all the activities that are born from within us. This is why a person can be spiritually satisfied without physical satisfaction. When using our creative genius the high will go on and on while physical ecstasy lasts but a moment. I am not discounting physical intimacy for it is wonderful, but it is the icing on the cake, not the cake itself. Don't "sell" your body and lose your self-love; only willingly give for love.

The true happiness and love we seek is found in the spiritual realm, not the physical one. Have you ever experienced an embrace so deep, without sensuousness, that your hearts literally felt as if they melted together as one, and you knew God's energy was there? This is real divine love. It is an eternal love. When two souls genuinely combine spiritual forces they actually generate the power of God. These partners know they are together to grow spiritually, as Marianne Williamson has so often stated. This eternal love is not physical and can exist on its own. If, however, physical intimacy has a deep spiritual connection first, it is a gift that knows no limits. Real love magically transforms each soul reflecting the enchantment of paradise.

The Masculine Code

As a woman I cannot fully comprehend who a man is, but from some tidbits of information I've gathered from my observations and notable "authorities" (men!), I can share some insights that might help in your desire for a partner. Let's have a little fun and find out what makes men who they are.

Men have been programmed throughout childhood just as we have been. Their programming has been with a masculine code to be in charge, to be tough, show no weakness, (big boys don't cry), become powerful and successful, be the protector, be a fixer, don't be emotional, and think logically. So men come into our lives with a wall already in place to ward off any hurts from us. In general they have not been "allowed" to show their emotions as little boys,

so cannot feel the emotions that we do.

Women are the nurturers. The seat of a woman's soul is her emotions. Her feelings are the most important aspect of her, and if a man wants to understand a woman he must understand this fact - emotions rule! Women have been known to use this emotional advantage in a manipulative way. You know - turn on the tears to get your way. Men don't like to see tears so it often works. But a woman who feels deeply is an asset when she comes from unconditional love. Manipulation is not part of her vocabulary and she is a blessing to her partner.

Men are the protectors; the seat of a man's soul is his intent or direction. Men are programmed to seek power and control to measure their own value by how much control they have, not how sensitive they are. Most men hate being vulnerable, so to protect themselves they often become "hunters." And what do they hunt? Women! Their egos tell them to put up their defenses so they cannot be hurt. This man avoids the emotional encounters that women need in their life. Men want admiration from us and want us to be proud of them.

Historically, in physical intimacy a man is more after physical gratification while a woman needs more of the emotional connection. But more men are opening up their hearts today because there is a spiritual awakening in our world. It's much more common to see a man weep in public, and how welcome a sight that is. They have feelings that need releasing as we do, and as they give themselves permission to express their emotions more openly, they are more willing to accept a woman of realness as they are becoming men of realness. I don't remember ever seeing my dad cry except for a few tears at his parent's funeral, and the same was true of my former husband. Fortunately my sons have expressed their emotions more easily at times and I'm grateful that they can do this. I was touched as I saw many men openly weep over a particularly sad part in a movie we were viewing not long ago. Yeah men!

Of course we can also find women who are closed and do not show their emotions. Such a woman has been deeply hurt and has erected a wall around her heart. We tend to close up after a hurtful experience. I remember once when I had a chakra test done after I had just been through a deeply hurtful experience and it showed my heart chakra was almost closed. I was really surprised because I have always been a caring person. I had to release some things and get that heart chakra open again because that's not a good place to be.

When two people become a "we" the identity of "me" and "thee" is often forgotten. From everything I have observed, experienced and read, the key to a wonderfully nurturing, loving and happy relationship is remaining the "me." The completeness of each individual as they stand for their truth and live their passion makes it a powerful relationship. Such a relationship is an unbeatable duo formed for God's glory, but in actuality it is a trio: "me," "thee" and God. This relationship is only of love and is formed to bring up wounds so they can heal. There is no armor in place as each partner is there for whatever the other must face, no matter how ugly and festering it is. Neither turns away from the other in their darkest hour; each partner is vulnerable as they unleash this darkness within them for their healing. Ironically, as each partner achieves their own identity, they can join together as one through love of God; there is no need.

Relationships formed for the glory of God know the realness of divine love. It is not need, but pure love. Your passion for life spills over into the passion you feel for your partner. It shines through Spirit and is a want, not a need. Your love is sufficient for yourself, but as Matt and Vicki ParClair say "*the more love there is, the more love there is*". You are love. You give love. Love is given to you. You are love. There is always love.

In closing, I pray that you understand your essence. Visualize yourself as a magnet. No matter what direction you move things are drawn to you. You have been created of God's design, a perfect being only of love. Why not build a bridge of love that reaches the far corners of the world and shines love to mankind. You are the essence of love and have the power as oneness with God. Take in these words from the song *Love Can Build a Bridge* - "*Love can build a bridge…between your heart and mine. Don't you think it's time.*"

It's time to wake up! Do you love your life as it is? If not, then you have to paint a different picture. You are a light that is needed to shine in the lighthouse to guide the world through the darkness. You have been called to light the way. It's time for you to break the limitations of your perception and become the powerhouse you are. It is your responsibility. No one can do your work but you. If you don't do it, who will?

When is the last time you bought yourself flowers? Love yourself enough to be treated to the beauty you are. I have done this repeatedly over the last few years for I love flowers and deserve to relish in their beauty. The day I knew this book would be completed, I bought myself two bouquets, one of which was yellow roses, a definite favorite. Every time I looked at them I *knew* my worth. Spoil yourself for you are worth it!

You are beautifully and wonderfully made, a woman of magnificence, rich beyond measure with God's treasures within you. How do you want to live your life? Everything you could ever imagine is yours if you believe. It's right there in your horizon, but you must choose to go after it and bring it to you. Let go of your worldly aspirations of the meaning of love and allow God's infinite, powerful, divine love to flood your heart, your soul and your being. Allow that love to shine forth all over the world. Be the light. Be the love. Just be…

A woman of worth, loving herself,
sharing love with those who cross her path,
for a moment, a passing space, or a lifetime.
You are priceless!

"The more love there is, the more love there is."

- Matt and Vicki ParClair

Review

1. Be the love you want.
It's the only way to attract the love you want.

⸙

2. There are not different kinds of love.
Love is all there is.

⸙

3. Relationships are not for fixing someone.
You cannot change anyone but yourself.

⸙

4. Use the exercise in stating what you want in a partner.
*Write the qualities you want in a partner and
send it out into the universe.*

⸙

5. Be yourself.
Don't try to be someone you're not. You will get found out.

⸙

6. Physical attraction
*Physical intimacy is never satisfied;
spiritual intimacy satisfies completely.*

⸙

7. Masculine code
*Men are protectors and have been taught not to show emotions.
Women are all about emotions.*

Empowerment Activity

Write the qualities you want in a partner or friend. After writing them, ask yourself if you are that value? If not, fix it!

_____   _____
_____   _____
_____   _____
_____   _____
_____   _____
_____   _____
_____   _____
_____   _____
_____   _____
_____   _____

Affirmation

_I choose to become pure, divine love and in
doing so, I am a woman of realness._

Open Up to Your Realness

Reflection

My purpose in writing this book was to open you to all that you are. I was given an urgent divine message to complete this rapidly, putting all other writings aside for a while. I was guided to complete it within three months; I completed it in ten weeks. I have learned to follow my guidance for there is a reason for its utterance.

I wrote this book to share my heart with yours. You, the reader, are the most important person in the world at this moment, for you and I are sharing our love. We are in a relationship, dancing together through love, each giving to the other. What a glorious moment. As you read this book the cycle is complete, in giving and receiving and giving again the never-ending circle of love.

I believe there are many messages throughout these pages that we all desperately need at this time in our lives. The words have been said before, sometimes in similar ways, but it seems we have not heard them. As the words flowed through me to this paper, I would often marvel at what my fingers had typed. I would see the very thing I needed to learn or remember because we always teach and share what we ourselves need to remember.

You have been made aware of old, negative patterns and unconscious recordings that have been playing not only in your mind, but recreating in your life experience, perhaps for your entire life. You can choose to hold onto them and continue the same song, or you can toss them away and open your hearts to a new voice.

The next chapters are to help you remember your magnificence and guide you with possibilities for growth as you become the person God intended you to be. There is no limit to the possibilities and all you must do is remember who you are.

The final section is devoted to being. It is time for you to be the light, to be the love, to be the miracle as you are one with the

Creator. You are born of love and are one with love, so your life is extraordinary as it brings you all the desires of your heart. It all begins within your being.

When the message came to write this book and the title was given to me, I had no idea what was coming next. I was divinely guided every step of the way by my guardian angel Hope and the host of angels that enlightened me with her. There is an awesomeness and holiness in the messages that are here, for they truly came from them through me. I feel honored to be God's instrument for sharing these truths.

Our time is now. The world is waiting. Are you ready to share your love? Are you the love?

Love Reflects Love

Carolyn

Appendix

Special Invitation

Carolyn Porter requests the honor of your presence for an incredible journey into the exciting dream adventure of a life-time. The journey has already begun and although it can change with your thoughts, it is never-ending. Please join your heart with hers and share in this momentous occasion. Just be love.

❧

To R.S.V.P.

Carolyn would love to hear from you as you travel on your life path. Contact her or for more information on her seminars, trainings, coaching sessions and products: www.drcarolynporter.com

Bibliography

Allen, James, *As A Man Thinketh,* Deseret Book Company, 2002, Salt Lake City, UT

Beattie, Melody, *Codependent No More,* Hazelden Publishing & Educational Services, 1987, Center City, MN

Beattie, Melody, *Beyond Codependency: and getting better all the time,* Harper & Row, Publishers, 1989, San Francisco, CA

Beck, Martha, *The Oprah Magazine,* June, 2003, Red Oak, IA

Breathnach, Sarah Ban, *Something More: Excavating Your Authentic Self,* Warner Books, Inc., 1998, New York, NY

Chopra, Deepak, *The Path to Love: Spiritual Strategies for Healing* Three Rivers Press, 1997, New York, NY

Cohen, Alan, *I Had It All the Time: When Self-Improvement Gives Way to Ecstasy,* Alan Cohen Publications, 1995, Haiku, HI

Ford, Debbie, *The Secret of the Shadow: The Power of Owning Your Story,* HarperCollins Publishers, 2002, Scranton, PA

Gordon, Richard, *Quantum Touch: The Power to Heal,* North Atlanta Books, 2002, Berkeley, CA

Hanh, Thich Nhat, *The Miracle of Mindfulness: A Manual on Meditation,* Beacon Press, 1976, Boston, MA

Jeffers, Susan, *End the Struggle and Dance with Life: How to Build Yourself Up When the World Gets You Down,* St. Martin's Griffin, 1997, New York, NY

Kahn, Dr. Jill, *The Gift of Taking: Honor Yourself First… All Else Will Follow,* Impressions Publishing, 2001, Marietta, GA

Peale, Dr. Norman Vincent, *The Power of Positive Thinking Ten Traits for Maximum Results,* Simon & Schuster Adult Publishing Group, 2003

Proctor, Robert, *You Were Born Rich,* LifeSuccess Productions, Inc., 1997, Phoenix, AZ

Richardson, Cheryl, *Life Makeovers: 52 Practical and Inspiring Ways to Improve Your Life One Week at a Time,* Broadway Books, 2002, New York, NY

Steindl-Rast, Brother David, *The Grateful Heart,* Sounds True, Incorporated, 1994

Vanzant, Iyanla, *One Day My Soul Just Opened Up: 40 Days and 40 Nights Towards Spiritual Strength and Personal Growth,* Simon & Schuster Adult Publishing Group, 1997

Whitfield, Dr. Charles, *Healing the Child Within: Discovery and Recovery for Adult Children of Dysfunctionsl Families,* Health Communications, Incorporated, 1987, Deerfield Beach, FL

Williamson, Marianne, *A Woman's Worth,* Random House, 1993, New York, NY

Winfrey, Oprah, *The Oprah Magazine,* July, 2003, Red Oak, IA

Zoehfeld, Kathleen W., *My Very First Winnie the Pooh Growing Up Stories,* Disney Press, 1999, New York, NY

About the Author

Carolyn Porter, D. Div., has discovered a new way of living as she began the process a few years ago of breaking through fear and becoming love. Her life has transformed and her desire is to empower you to do the same. She is a speaker, trainer and wholeness coach who is known for her ability to reach out and touch your heart so that your heart opens to your own greatness.

Carolyn began with a long, successful career as a piano instructor of hundreds of students in her own piano studio. She is the mother of five and attributes much of her success from the interaction, understanding and love of her children - three daughters and two sons. After becoming ill and discovering alternative methods of healing, she opened several health stores with her sons. She has touched many lives with her knowledge and caring heart, and is continuing to share and give through her speaking, coaching and writing. She lives in Atlanta, Georgia.

More from Carolyn Porter

Books
A Woman's Path to Wholeness: The Gift is in the Process
The Realness of a Woman

✺

Audio
Grab Your Authentic Power

✺

Sharing Our Gifts
A Woman of Worth double-matted poem
Sharing Our Gifts greeting cards

✺

Also
Life Skills Speaking Program
Life Skills Coaching Program
Seminars
Workshops

The above books are available through your local bookstore or
through our website.

Please visit our website for additional information at
www.drcarolynporter.com